THE BEST OF NORTH AMERICAN HUNTER

For the Love of Hunting

❖   ❖   ❖   ❖   ❖

Minnetonka, Minnesota

The Best of North American Hunter
For the Love of Hunting

Printed in 2005.

Tom Carpenter
Creative Director

Heather Koshiol
Book Development Coordinator

Greg Schwieters
Book Design and Production

Laura Belpedio
Book Development Assistant

Gregg Gutschow
Gordy Krahn
Mike Faw
Steve Bauer
Cory Pedersen
North American Hunter Staff

4 5 6 7 8 / 08 07 06 05
ISBN 1-58159-164-0
© 2002 North American Hunting Club

North American Hunting Club
12301 Whitewater Drive
Minnetonka, MN 55343
www.huntingclub.com

Photo Credits
Grady Allen 54, 72, 80, 95; **Kenny Bahr** 28, 101 (B); **Mike Barlow** 132; **George Barnett** 125; **Chuck Bartlett** 147, 148; **Rebecca Bradford** 8, 9; **Denver Bryan** 110 (bobcat); **Gary Clancy** 38; **Judd Cooney** 14, 75, 96 (left), 129; **John Ford** 86, 97, 102; **Michael H. Francis** 57, 58; **Green Agency/Bill Buckley** 1, 98, 100, 103, 104, 109; **Green Agency/Dusan Smetana** 1; **J. Chris Hansen** 61; **Don Jones** cover onlay, 1, 34, 43, 53, 74, 76, 118, 121, 133 (top center), 138, 152; **Mark Kayser** 29, 41, 42, 50 (top & bottom), 68, 69 (inset), 69, 106, 107, 110 (red fox), 114, 115, 117 (left & right), 120 (right), 130, 134, 143, 144, 145; **Mitch Kezar** 120 (center); **Bill Kinney** 37, 48, 142; **Lee Kline** 25, 26, 66, 84; **Gary Kramer** 131, 150; **Lance Krueger** 12, 15, 122, 124 (bottom), 126 (bottom); **Barbara Leibell** 27; **Bill Marchel** 88, 89, 90, 92, 93, 101(C), 101(D), 101 (E), 101(F); **Steve Maslowski** 110 (gray fox); **Neil Mishler** 101 (A); **Bob Noonan** 13; **Mark Raycroft** 55; **Bob Robb** 46, 139, 141; **Mike Searles** 72 (inset); **Jim Shockey** 16, 18 (all), 19 (all), 20, 21, 62 (top), 64, 65, 151; **Dusan Smetana** 99; **Ron Spomer** 63, 110 (coyote); **Wayne van Zwoll** 120 (left), 121 (inset), 124 (top), 126 (top); **Bill Vaznis** 1, 4; **Rick Vincunas** 94; **Mark Werner** 128; **Wild Wings Gallery** 79; **Remaining photographs property of NAHC:** 6, 11, 16 (inset), 22-23, 31, 39, 45, 51 (top & bottom), 59, 60, 62 (bottom), 70, 71, 73, 77, 78, 82, 83, 85, 96, 108, 111, 113, 127, 133 (inset, bottom, top left & top right), 135, 136, 137, 153.

❖ CONTENTS ❖

THE BEST OF NORTH AMERICAN HUNTER

For the Love of Hunting

As a member of the North American Hunting Club, you receive the best hunting magazine there is: *North American Hunter*. Great writing, super photography, hunting topics of high interest, issues of great importance—Gordy Krahn, Dave Maas, Steve Bauer and Cory Pedersen combine their personal talents to pull it all together into packages that are beautiful to behold, informative to read and worth saving.

But magazines often get lost in the shuffle. They go to deer camp (or turkey, elk or duck camp). They get lent to a friend and don't find their way back. Or, after being read, they pile up with everything else, and the whole stack ends up in the recycling bin.

That's understandable. Life today is busy. And you can't save everything forever. But the contents of *North American Hunter*—the stories, the tales, the tactics and techniques and tips—are timeless. So we had an idea, a great idea: Create a book that utilizes the best of the club's magazine material, doing our best to do it justice, and present it to members as a special keepsake edition.

You're holding the result of one year: *The Best of North American Hunter—For the Love of Hunting*.

Here is a collection of some of *North American Hunter's* very best feature articles, all wrapped up into one convenient, handsome and permanent package.

We lead with a chapter called "For the Love of Hunting," a collection of stories exploring the essence of our hunting passion: why we do it, how much it means to us, and how much we love the people we choose to do it with. In fact, the book is named after this important chapter.

Of course, you want to continue to expand your hunting horizons and skills too, so chapters on hunting deer, turkeys, birds and upland game, and big game beyond deer, follow.

This is an exciting book—worth the effort to create, and worth the price to have at your disposal for as long as you want.

May all your days afield be good ones!

Tom Carpenter
Editor—North American Hunting Club Books

FOR THE LOVE OF HUNTING

We live in an age when hunting isn't necessary for our physical survival; we can purchase sustenance at the grocery store or a restaurant.

But hunting is an emotional necessity. It connects you with places and things that are still wild. It offers action, excitement and the opportunity for accomplishment. It is intense. It is a time to be by yourself—to reflect on and inspect what is in your hunter's heart. And it is a time to be with people that matter—yes, dare it be said, people we love.

It is this passion, this longing for the chase, that brings a hunter together and makes him or her whole. And a love of hunting also brings people together in some of life's most meaningful relationships.

❖ Of Love & Hunting ❖

By Rebecca Bradford

High on a mountaintop last season, a client brought up the curious passion he feels for hunting and he said that hunting was the one true love in his life. It got me thinking about the remarkable similarities between love and hunting, and the way that so many people feel that they have to sacrifice one for the other. Hunting and love. I know that one of my true loves is hunting.

I know that I prepared for years to become a hunting guide. I know that I've spent sleepless nights and shed tears over the pursuit of game. I know that nothing can get my blood boiling like an argument about the mountains and conservation and my desire to appreciate the same living that my grandparents did. I've worn the skin off my feet, the retinas off my eyes and the fat off my body for hunting. I remember the years of being the camp brat, cleaning the mess of eyeballs and brains for the guides—those magical creatures who would plop down their game, caress the annuli on a sheep horn and then walk off on the next hunt, their footprints mere ripples on water.

I cannot count the number of times that I rose in the dark from my bough bed and followed deceitful, fleeing horsetracks with my flashlight, ears aching for the echo of horse bells, only to return at dawn in time to cook breakfast. And I was grateful to have the honor of building the fire, boiling the coffee and breathing smoke over cast-iron pans. Just to get to go on a hunt. I was never too tired to follow the hunters up the hill with a packboard three sizes too large, stuffed with lunches not my own. You cannot maintain this level of physical and mental hardship unless you are in love.

When I was finally guiding, I remember sleepless nights, worrying. Under a hunter's moon on the trail, picturing the rams on the hill, tracing their paths in my mind, imagining the different scenarios of capture. Feeling the wind change, changing the plan, planning the alternatives. Worrying. Listening for horsebells, leaping awake with a start when I hadn't heard them for too long. Worrying. Like love, it can consume you.

The phenomenon mentioned by my client is that the passion for love and hunting can feel so similar at times. There is that same adrenaline rush when you see your quarry. The strong role fate can play in both pursuits, like the chance encounter in a coffee shop and a ram rising out of the mist as you cross the same trail. That your paths crossed at the same time seems destiny. That you were lucky enough to get what you hunted is a miracle. The role that coincidence plays in both. The way that your heart pounds as you sense your prey just over the next rise, or smell the warm musky scent of sheep on the breeze, or hear rocks rolling down the canyon as you frantically scan the slide with your eyes. The way that all your senses are heightened during a hunt. The immense, brokenhearted feeling when you miss and watch the animal disappear. The way that your mind will run the film of failure over. The way that you wonder what you could have done differently. The

Only if you're in love—with hunting—can you maintain the level of physical and mental hardship it takes to succeed.

way that you always remember "the one that got away."

I have had hunters tell me that their partners or children do not share their love for hunting. I have had these same hunters phone me at 3 a.m. in December from 2,000 miles away and begin the conversation with, "Do you remember when ... ?"

Perhaps it was the fog and the melancholy weather. Perhaps the discussion was prompted by the fact that we—guide, wrangler and hunter—were holed up beneath a massive granite boulder on the top of a mountain pass, waiting for the fog to clear with nothing else to do. This hunter told me that he believed that there was room in a person's heart for only one true love, and

that for him that love was hunting. He told me that there has never been another love that has made him feel this way. He sounded so very alone.

The worst of it was that he was not the first to have said such things. I will never cease to be amazed at the power of the mountaintop confessional to remind me of how fortunate I am that the people who I care about the most appreciate the outdoors the same way that I do.

You cannot deny your roots. Genetically, we are all hunters; it is how our species survived. If you loved hunting from a young age, share it with your partner. If it is love, then it is worth it. If you are in love with hunting and the outdoors and all that it entails, then you had better make sure that the person with whom you spend your life can share that same love. If you are lucky enough or smart enough to do this, then your pleasure will be enhanced 10-fold. The alternative is to lead a lonely existence.

Encourage your partner or your family to share the rare beauty that the hunt can bring, from the early morning campfire coffee to the breathtaking view of a pristine mountain valley. Take the people you love to the places that so few get to see. Some of the happiest, most content couples I've ever seen have been those I took hunting. Some of the most enviable parent/child relationships were between those who came to the mountains ostensibly in pursuit of big game, but who were really looking to spend time and experiences together. Don't get defensive when your loved ones demand that you choose. Take them along. Give them an opportunity to share your love.

Love. Be it hunting, someone's heart, race car driving or golf. Choose carefully. The fury with which and the people with whom we pursue our dreams will determine the depth of their footprints in the hills and valleys of our memory. ❖

❖ WALKING HOME ❖

By James Krause

It had been years since I had been up there, but I agreed to go as a favor to my father. Despite accepting the offer to deer hunt with my family, I was convinced that my indifferent feelings would not change. During my college years, I had drifted away from the hunting lifestyle.

I could tell, however, during our opening night dinner, that my dad was happy to have his three sons in camp, even though the day was unsuccessful. He and his father, who had been his only hunting partner, hunted for years out of a two-bunk trailer hidden deep in the northern woods. Even a stroke, years before Grampa Walt's death in 1978, was not enough to keep him from hunting. A year after Grampa died, my dad hauled the trailer up north and hunted alone. After that, it was never used again.

The second day of the season was quiet until a twig snapped. A buck was slinking through a poplar stand; his brown, 5-point rack contrasting with the snow. He was heading toward one small opening in the thicket.

I eased my rifle to my shoulder and waited. I followed him through my scope until I was sure that I had a clear shot. As the buck stepped into the opening, it looked in my direction. I paused for a moment when I stared into his black eyes, before squeezing the trigger.

I ran to find what I thought would be a heavy blood-trail. Instead, I found an inch-thick poplar split in half, 10 feet in front of the deer's last visible position. I searched in vain for any sign of a hit. There was no blood, hair or break in stride—a clean miss.

Upset that I could have crippled the deer, I questioned what I was doing in the woods. But I recalled my excitement as this lucky buck nosed its way past me. I even had faint memories of my first deer—a button buck—and how it felt to kneel next to it and greet my father with a smile. I could not reconcile the miss, but I could admit that I had at one time loved hunting.

Throughout that season, my father and I spent our lunches walking fire trails together and talking. It wasn't the same shallow talk or heated arguments, however, that we'd had when I was a teenager; it was like two old friends meeting again after years of separation. Old grudges were forgotten in favor of catching up and discovering that neither of us was such bad a guy after all.

After one particularly moving walk, I continued wandering those stark fire trails. After several hours, I crossed a bobcat track where it had stalked a rabbit into a swampy creekbottom. As I placed my thumb in the frosted cat track, an old memory of my dad kneeling next to a deer track filled my consciousness. He patiently explained that its depth, shape and width held secrets. All I could think at the time was how grown-up I felt and how proud I was to be there. Now, 14 years later, I was saddened that the childlike wonder that I felt welling up inside was tempered by the realization that I almost let it slip away into the ether of time.

At the cabin, we told stories into the night. My brothers and I wanted to hear about the past, and Dad obliged.

"Grampa loved deer hunting. He shot a buck more years than not when he was younger," he said proudly, as if it was the first time he had uttered the words. "That buck on the wall was shot in a blizzard with that old .32 Special Winchester that I bring up every year."

"How old was I when you shot your last buck?" I asked. "I can barely remember it."

"Oh, jeez," he replied. "I think it was 1977, so you were 5 or 6. It was that 4-pointer that had a chipped drop tine. That broke a long luckless streak for us. Grampa came over the hill waving his arms. The stroke raised holy hell with his speech so he didn't say a lot. He just kept patting me on the back saying, 'Good ... good ... good!' I think he was happier than I was.

"After his stroke, I think that it was hard for him to hunt. It would've been easier on him to stay at home like Gramma wanted him to, but he loved it too much and wanted me to keep hunting. It was important to him that I never walk away from deer hunting. And if I hunted, he wanted to be there with me, even if it killed him. It meant so much to him to be out there together that he had tears running down his cheeks when we dragged my buck out of the woods. He knew that it was his last season. He kept shaking his head and patting me on the back all night and ..."

After a long pause he added, "He loved this so much, guys. I wish that he could be here to tell you himself." We sat in silence for several long minutes.

I found myself staring at an old picture that night. Two men, my grandfather and his brother, stood next to a 1955 Chevy station wagon. On top of the car were two massive deer. I recognized one of them as the deer on our cabin wall.

"Read the back of that picture," my dad said.

On the back, in faded ink, was written: "We really missed you this year, son. Maybe you'll decide to join us next year. Dad '59."

Those faded words made me realize that deer hunting is less of a blood sport defined by death than it is a celebration of life despite death. When the alarm woke everyone else at 4:30 on the final morning of the hunt, I knew that I'd never miss another season.

As the day wore on, minutes melted into hours that continued to click away without incident. I didn't even ready my gun when a doe settled in front of me, or when the ghostly apparition that followed her sifted through the fog and disappeared.

The phantom deer had circled downwind of the doe and dangerously close to me. For the longest seconds of the day, it stood there content to wait out the daylight hours in a jungle of saplings and brush, teasing me with its closeness. In the past, I would've thrown the gun up and hoped for the best. Today, though, I was happy just to be there.

When it ducked its head and stared at me, I had to look back. After a hair-thin moment, the deer's identity registered in my cloudy head: Buck! In increments that were something less than perceptible movement, I lifted my grandfather's tiny .32 Special lever action to my shoulder. I leveled the front hooded sight with the rear ram's horn on the patch of light-brown hair on the deer's shoulder.

Scores of old photos with

smiling hunters, old cars and deer clogged my senses. The forest held its breath. The fog thickened as if an audience of old deer hunters' ghosts assembled to see what I would do next. I swear that I felt a hand on my shoulder when I squeezed the trigger.

There would be no blood trail to follow. It was an 8-point buck, wider than the old mount in the cabin, but lacking the mass and character. As I stared at my tiny silhouette in the deer's eye, I thought of the past five days. Those days faded into the past 19 years; in particular, the deer seasons and Grampa's funeral when I was six.

Minutes later, in the dark, I knelt in the snow as steam rose from my outstretched, blood-smeared hands. In the beam of my flashlight, I quietly spoke to the deer, thanking it. When the headlights of our truck burned through the fog, I was truly sorry that the hunt was over.

"I wish that you were here, Grampa," I thought as I stood to greet my family.

When we were packing to go home the next day, I found myself standing in the shadow of my deer as it hung on our buck pole.

"It's a beauty," my dad said, patting me on the back.

"Why didn't you ever give up on me, Dad?" I asked.

"Because you love deer hunting too much, and I didn't want you to forget that. Are you going to be here next year?"

"I'd like to," I said, staring into the buck's cloudy eyes.

"We'd be glad to have you."

All I could think to say as melting snow dripped from the roof to the ground was, "Thanks, Dad." ❖

❖ BUCK WALK ❖

By Bob Noonan

Just before daybreak in mid-November, a pickup truck carrying Charlie Yanush and two friends bounced along a dirt road through Maine's spruce and fir wilderness near Moosehead Lake. This area is known for huge whitetails.

"A buck jumped up out of a creekbottom on the left and crossed the road in front of us," Charlie told me. "He was a big boy all right, with heavy antlers. He disappeared into some thick firs on the right. We stopped and I grabbed my rifle and jumped out. We had about 6 inches of new, wet snow; perfect for tracking."

Charlie and I were sitting in his trophy room in Greenfield, Maine, swapping deer hunting stories. Charlie has been a professional guide in Alaska for 13 years, five of them with famous master guide, Lynn Castle. But here in his home state, he's best known as a consistently successful hunter of large white-tailed bucks. Heavy-beamed racks hang from the walls and rafters in his garage.

"I walk them down," Charlie said. "I find a fresh buck track early in the morning and stay on it all day until I get a shot. Tracks don't come much earlier or fresher than the ones I watched that buck make," he said with a laugh.

At dawn, Charlie stepped into the evergreens and loaded his .30-06. The buck had run for only a short distance before slowing to an unconcerned walk. Charlie followed.

The tracks entered a swamp full of hummocks of alders and swale grass about 150 yards wide. On the right side was a clear-cut filled with young second-growth firs, raspberry bushes and slash piles. On the left, the swamp was bordered by tall, mature spruce. A quarter-mile into the timber, a 50-foot-high knoll rose abruptly out of the flat terrain.

The buck began meandering as soon as it entered the swamp. "He had no idea that I was behind him," Charlie said. "There were pools of water everywhere between the hummocks and some ice; the kind that almost supports you, then breaks when you put your full weight on it. I soon went in over the tops of my knee-high rubber boots. It was a warm day, mid-30s, overcast, with a light drizzle. It was perfectly calm, absolutely no wind, very quiet."

A small stream, about 5 feet wide and knee-deep, meandered through the swamp. The buck sailed across easily. Charlie hunted for a narrow spot, jumped over and backtracked to pick up the track.

And so it went. The buck crossed the stream repeatedly, zigzagging through the swamp, browsing, and Charlie labored patiently behind, searching for crossings, picking up the track again, always fighting brush and water. For three hours he neither saw, nor heard, the deer.

He was on the right side of the stream when he heard

He knows you're there.

a commotion on the opposite side, less than 100 yards away. Branches crashed and antlers banged antlers.

"Had to be my boy fighting another one," Charlie said. "The stream had widened and I couldn't find a place to cross, so I built a bridge out of dead alders. It was none too solid so I crawled across on my belly to distribute my weight. I headed for the racket."

A thick band of alders surrounded the swamp. Charlie pushed carefully through. He stopped at the edge and peered into the spruce. It was fairly open under the 2-foot-thick trunks.

Three does were staring at him, only 10 yards away.

"I froze," Charlie said. "Then I made out other deer, all staring at me. Tails started twitching, then they all took off, flags flopping everywhere. As best I could tell, there were eight of them. I saw at least two racks."

The ground was torn up, with some blood and hair on the snow. Tracks were everywhere. Charlie sorted them out, looking for his buck.

"I found him pretty quickly," he said. "The others left together, in the same direction. His was the only set leaving in a different direction and they were by far the biggest. You can almost always depend on the big guy leaving by himself."

The buck ran a short distance, then resumed walking. He headed back in the direction that he'd come, but toward the spruce, not the swamp. Charlie followed patiently.

The buck gradually swung in a wide circle toward the knoll. When he reached it, he went along the back edge.

Charlie stopped at the base and looked up. Twenty yards away, he saw hair. Seconds later, tails bounced off.

"I'd spooked them again!" He said with disgust. "I ran up the slope and found 8 or 10 beds in the knee-high jack firs, the stunted stuff under the timber. The big guy had joined them, and once again he headed off in a different direction, back toward the fight area."

This time the buck ran a good 100 yards and then trotted a considerable distance before stopping.

"The second time that I jump them," Charlie said, "I run when they do, to keep up. I don't let them get more than a quarter-mile ahead. When they break down to a trot, I move to a fast walk.

"When they stop trotting, they'll usually stop and look back over their trail. Often, they'll circle to a good vantage point in cover, like behind a blow-down or in a thicket. They'll stop for about 5 or 10 minutes. If they see nothing coming, they relax and start their zigzag browsing again," Charlie said.

"This is a basic behavioral pattern that I've seen for years," he continued. "Pretty much the same all the time.

"When I find where they've stepped around to watch their trail, I start sneaking. I'm hunting now, trying to see them first. I go 20 or 30 yards, then stop to look and listen. Don't always expect them to be ahead of you; most of the time they'll be to the right or left. Before you leave, look behind. Always watch behind.

"I might get a shot, but this early in the game I'll most likely jump him again."

The buck came back to his and Charlie's tracks leaving the fight area and jumped into them, following

Maine whitetail hunter Charlie Yanush persistently tracks big bucks, looking for a showdown.

them back toward the knoll. He left the trail several times and milled around, watching his backtrack. But each time, he returned to the tracks and moved on.

"Typical behavior," Charlie said. "By now, he suspected that he was being followed."

The buck followed the tracks back to the knoll. The other deer had returned and he rejoined them on top.

"When big deer are being followed, they like to mingle with others," Charlie said. "They're probably hoping that you'll lose their tracks amongst the rest. Plus, there's safety in numbers; all those eyes watching."

Charlie plodded up the slope and jumped the deer a third time.

"This time, I definitely saw three sets of antlers," he told me. "I had a halfway decent shot at what I thought was my buck, but I let him go because I wasn't sure."

Once again, the buck backtracked down off the knoll. When he came to where he first joined their tracks leaving the fight area, he rejoined them again, circling back to the knoll.

"The buck was staying in a small area and that's unusual," Charlie said.

"Normally, they head out in a fairly straight line when they're pushed. They move along, no more browsing. They want to put distance between you and them."

The buck stopped several times to watch the trail behind him. Charlie made a decision.

"By now it was past noon, and when they stop more often, they start getting more careless. So I stopped sneaking and walked along. I was pushing him now."

The tactic had immediate results. The buck left the trail and angled to the left, away from the knoll. His trail went fairly straight for a quarter-mile, through mixed growth, stopping twice more to look back. Finally, the deer came to an old, partially grown-up clear-cut and headed into it.

The cut was a tangled mixture of chest-high brush piles and thorny raspberry vines, with almost impenetrable patches of fir, spruce saplings and hardwood suckers. The mess was a good 150 yards wide and ended against a solid wall of young evergreens.

Charlie waded in. The buck's path was obvious. His belly dragged where he jumped brush piles and he knocked snow off the evergreens where he barged through. Charlie threaded his way behind, sometimes on hands and knees, branches slapping his face, snow sliding onto him.

Halfway across, he crawled under a brushy log and stood up for a look.

The buck was standing stock-still in the open against the evergreens, staring at Charlie.

"Eventually, they get careless," Charlie said. "I think that they're weary. I jump them more often. They start looking back from more open places, like from the side of a hardwood ridge, or from the other side of a stream. They seem to think that water is a barrier.

"And they stand longer. It's almost as if they want to get a good look at you and figure out what's going on. They run shorter distances and don't try to hide as much as they run. Sooner or later, I get a clear, close-standing shot, almost always within 30 yards."

Charlie brought his rifle up, and the buck bolted. Incredibly, he charged at the hunter.

"He ran low and straight out; he never jumped," Charlie said. "How the hell he got through that mess I don't know, he just bulldozed through. He was in and out of sight and I could only see antlers coming. I could hear him though. He angled to the left and passed by me within 20 yards. I aimed under his antlers and fired twice as soon as his body was visible. He kept going."

There was no blood or hair. Charlie pushed on.

The buck headed toward the knoll and got back into the trail that he and Charlie had made on their three trips around the big mound. By now, the trail was a mixture of confused tracks. Charlie stopped to decipher them.

There were two fresh sets on top of each other, going in opposite directions.

At first, Charlie thought that there was another deer. A closer look revealed that it was the same one, backtracking. He followed the set leading away to the left.

Within 30 yards, the trail entered thick, 4-foot-high firs. Abruptly, the new tracks ended.

"It's a favorite tactic," Charlie said. "They'll back-track on their own or the hunter's tracks, or both, and then they'll circle to watch the trail from the side. Big deer, in particular, will make a big leap to the side, into thick stuff to shake you. So I circled, too. I made three loops before I picked him up. He'd made a standing leap of more than 20 feet."

The buck headed back toward the cut and crossed it again, near where he had crossed it the first time. Charlie followed, crashing through, abandoning all attempts at silence. It was 3:30 p.m., and the early November twilight was deepening. Less than an hour of shooting light remained.

Halfway across, Charlie saw the buck standing at the edge of the evergreens. He raised his rifle. The buck leaped into the evergreens.

This time, he only made a few jumps before walking. Charlie pushed ahead and jumped him again within 30 yards. A short distance later, he saw the big deer standing there.

"He turned and I had a decent rear-end shot, but I didn't take it. When he left, I followed slowly. I figured that the end was near."

Charlie soon saw a brown body standing broadside. He crosshaired the shoulders and got ready to pull.

The deer lowered its head. No antlers!

The doe jumped, exposing a bigger deer behind her. Charlie glimpsed a rack as the buck ran off.

"The doe had been bedded," he said. "The tracks looked like he had got her up and put her between us. I'm convinced that he did it deliberately, to sacrifice her and mislead me."

The buck's tracks headed deeper into the firs, then circled. He was headed back to the clear-cut. It was now almost too dark to shoot under the evergreens. Charlie made a split second decision; he ran like hell for the cut. If the buck-crossed first he would be gone.

Charlie broke into the open and heard crashing coming through the evergreens to his right. He took off on a dead run along the edge of the cut, toward the noise.

He stopped to gulp air and there was the buck, standing 20 feet back in the evergreens. Charlie had cut him off.

By getting on a buck's trail early in the day and relentlessly tracking him, the payoff might be a close shot at a trophy animal.

"He was facing me, his front legs spread wide, his head low, staring. He looked angry. I didn't even think. I put the crosshairs at the top of his brisket, at the base of his neck, and squeezed the trigger."

The buck dropped like a rock.

Back at Charlie's, I examined the skull and heavy-beamed 10-point rack. "Nice deer," I offered.

"Not bad," Charlie agreed. "Dressed out at 248 pounds.

"You won't catch up with all of them," he said. "But if you get on them early and stay with them, chances are good that they'll eventually give you a shot. Maybe they're tired of being pushed around. Some act like they want to have a showdown."

Which Charlie is happy to provide. ❖

❖ DIARY OF DESPAIR ❖
THE STORY OF A POLAR BEAR HUNT IN THE ARCTIC

By Jim Shockey

March 1 - The first day of my polar bear hunt! Sort of. I'm on the first airborne leg of the trip; I'll be flying all night and most of tomorrow.

March 2 - Arrived safely at 4 p.m. (with my Knight muzzleloader intact!) at my final destination, Hall Beach, in the new Canadian territory of Nunavut. My good friend, Fred Webb, is the outfitter, and I met Ike Angotautok, the head guide and Daniel Kaunak, the assistant guide. James Kukkik is the dog musher. From what I understand, he is already on the ice with the dog team.

March 3 - We're on the tundra! I got my polar bear tag at noon, and we headed out. We traveled as far as Hall Lake today and are staying in Daniel's father's tiny plywood shack tonight.

I've been riding on the back of the sled "komitick," pulled by a snow machine. Rough doesn't describe the ride, although it's smoother than my Pre '94 "Mighty" Dodge.

March 4 - Caught up with James today. It's been blizzarding for the past two days here on the Melville Peninsula. James has been sitting in a canvas lean-to, waiting out the storm. It's ugly, zero visibility, but they say that we'll try to make it across to the Gulf of Boothia tomorrow. Didn't John Franklin and his crew disappear there? My fingers are cold but crossed, and my hopes high. Tonight will be the first night in the canvas tent.

March 5 - Made it to the ice today! We hit saltwater at the mouth of Garry Bay. We set up the tent beside a small, rocky island, right at the edge of the "rough ice." Not exactly what I expected; there's no going farther out into the Gulf. The bears will have to come to us. No open water and no seals, just truck-sized slabs of ice jumbled up as far as you can see.

March 6 - First bear sighting! James and I traveled on the dogsled north nearly 15 miles. Temperature was minus 35. As we searched for an opening in the rough ice, we spotted a sow and last year's cub. Unbelievable! We watched her for an hour and then set up camp for the night. James says that a boar will be following her.

March 7 - Evil luck today. James and I left camp early on the dogsled while Ike and Daniel lounged in the tent. At noon, a monster 9-foot bear lumbered right into camp and terrorized them! They had to shoot five times into the ice at its feet to make it back off. Even

It could have ended right here. The second day of the hunt, this giant polar bear terrorized camp. But Shockey and his guide were a mile away. By the time they returned, the bear was gone. Inset: The hunt area.

then, it only backed 30 feet from the tent! The facts were written in the tracks.

By the time James and I returned, the bear was gone. Like I said, evil luck.

March 8 - We rested today. James thought that the bear might come back, so we stayed in camp. I glassed all morning and have apparently burned my eyeballs. My left eye is now snow-blind. It feels like sand and nails are in it. It's going to take a couple of days to heal, I think.

March 9 - We moved on today; James and I on the dogsled and the others on snow machines. We stopped after 10 or so miles and set up camp. Low, blowing snow this morning, not too bad, about minus 30. The stove and lantern are our only heat, and we keep both going all night.

With my hunt past the halfway point, I'll recap some details:

Lunch is usually raw walrus, raw caribou or "Mr. Noodle." Tonight we ate boiled walrus. Last night we had boiled caribou.

Having trouble with my saboted bullets. The first two practice shots went totally haywire because of the sabot freezing and blowing apart, I believe. Now I'm trying to keep the gun warm on the dogsled by wrapping it in my sleeping bag and stuffing the bag full of disposable handwarmers. Thank you, Hot Hands!

There are 14 dogs in the team, four pups and 10 adults. James uses a 30-foot whip, too often for my liking. I'm usually kneeling on the dogsled, and the fresh snow screeches, and whines and complains as the sled drags over it at about 3 mph. James yells directions to the lead dog in Inook. So far, we have only broken one snow machine. No problem, they roped the undercarriage together. Now it's fine.

The ice is extremely rough. Ten-foot-thick chunks of ice, some of them as tall and wide as a house, stand on edge and sideways all stacked up and ugly. Under this jumble are cracks and seal holes. That's what polar bears search for. So far, we've only found a couple of seal holes, dens actually, where they make little caverns underneath the snow. They come up to breathe and then lie on the ice underneath the snow. The lack of seal sign is disturbing. Not only does it mean that polar bears

won't be here, it means that we haven't harpooned a seal for dog food yet. The dogs are already on half-rations. I suspect that we're next.

The idea, as I understand it, is to set up a base camp when we find a lot of bear sign. Then we'll hunt from there in each direction; so far we are still looking. Nights have been clear. The northern lights have been rare, only one night that I know of.

The moon is a silver sliver in the dark sky, and Ike tells me that when it's tipped on its side like it is, it holds lots of animals. It's supposed to be a good time to hunt. At least that's what Inuit legend would have you believe. We'll see.

I have every inch of my flesh covered during the day on the dogsled and still have impressive black frost burns across my forehead and on my nose. James wears nothing on his face. Unbelievable! These guys don't appear to get cold. A shower here consists of a small tin can with a string on the top, attached to a nail that hangs on the tent ridgepole, about 4 feet off the ice. There are holes cut in the can so that you can fill it with hot water. Then you let it drip on you as you kneel under it on the ice. So far I haven't had a shower because I don't think that I smell. Everyone suggests that perhaps my nose isn't working properly.

I've learned that dog fur is the best kind for making parkas and mukluks. It apparently doesn't frost up and is better than wolf or wolverine. I decided that there isn't much of a future being a sled dog up here.

My toothpaste and toothbrush are frozen. Deodorant is a lot of fun to put on in the morning. Since I don't smell, however, I don't use it.

In the tent and in my sleeping bag I wear long johns, a sweater, wool pants and a jacket. I'm always cold unless I get into my sleeping bag or the guys crank the stove up. That doesn't happen often because we're already short of gas.

March 10 - I fell up to my thighs in a seal den today. Just missed falling into the water by inches. Close call.

I also fell off the dogsled and rammed both shins onto the edge of an ice block. I'm now lying here with an ice pack on each shin; at least it's no problem finding ice up here. I just chip it from our floor. The lump on one shin is the size of a grapefruit, but it could have

Glassing for polar bears is the ultimate test of binoculars and human eyes in the blinding cold (left). Below two photos, one of many ugly days in the arctic when all one can do is hunker down and hope to survive.

been worse. Last spring, a hunter got his fingers caught over the edge of the sled and sliced a couple of them off. The dogs pull slowly, but with incredible force.

It was bitter cold today, coldest day yet because of the wind; easily minus 70 or 80 counting the windchill.

Unbelievably, water isn't easy to come by up here. Lots of snow, but it takes too much of our gas to melt enough for coffee, so the guys look for old, blue freshwater icebergs. The ice under us is too salty to use for drinking.

Glassing for bears is nearly impossible. The instant you lift your binos, they fog because of your body heat.

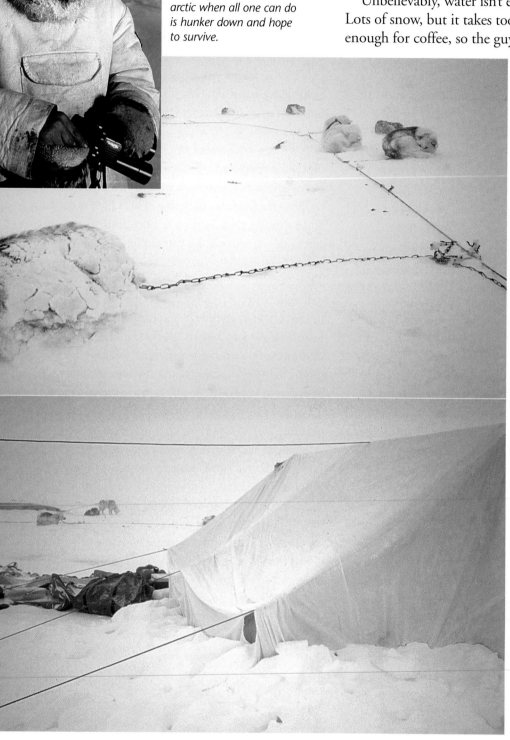

March 11 - My frostbite is getting worse. Apparently, if you get it really bad, your whole nose turns black and falls off. Nice. Three people in Hall Beach have amputations because of frostbite. One old fellow lost both of his legs while walrus hunting. He was lucky; his two hunting buddies froze to death.

I must be getting clumsier as I get more run down from the constant cold. I fell off the sled again today; the whole thing tipped over on me. Another close call.

Very disappointing; didn't find any fresh tracks today. No seals. Nothing. We're down to the last meal of walrus. I'm sure that they'll be upset once they run out.

Today was the toughest day on the dogsled. It just seemed to go on forever, slow and right into the wind.

March 12 - The seventh hunting day and again clear, beautiful skies. Aren't we lucky? The fire went out during the night, so my gun is frozen again. As it thaws out, of course, the frost melts into waterfalls down the barrel and onto the powder. I'm going to have to reload again. This cold weather is wreaking havoc on my equipment.

We actually camped in relative luxury tonight because we're on top of snow instead of ice. That meant that we could dig down about 14 inches to make a bed shelf for our sleeping bags. We can sit with our feet down; almost like sitting in a chair! Luxury is a relative thing here. Today the sled runners screeched when they crossed the snow. It was like listening to 1,000 people scratching their fingernails on a chalkboard for eight hours straight. Dismal hunting. No tracks. It's getting harder to stay positive.

March 15 - Two days without luck. Another morning. Ike is leaving today to go back for supplies. I'm staying, however, because I enjoy it out here. Right.

Last night we feasted on boiled char—head, guts and all ...

Wow! A polar bear just wandered through camp! Just when everything seemed so hopeless! Unfortunately, it was small. Twice it approached, and they had to shoot into the snow at its feet. Got some great video footage!

March 16 - Fourteen days on the ice. Ike should be near Hall Beach. Today we're not going anywhere, I guess. I'd have to say that we're getting low on most

things at this point. I'm supposed to be on an airplane today, going home.

No fresh tracks around camp last night. Nothing, no hope. We're still waiting. We'll see what happens.

I stood outside the tent today for a bit. It's absolutely desolate, ice all around. The ice pops and groans. Once in a while a crackling roar passes like a wave. I guess the tides create a pressure edge, crushing the ice against itself. What a forbidding place.

He's not stuck or trying to hide. Instead, one of Shockey's native guides searches seal holes for fresh seal sign. Find seals and you find polar bears.

March 17 - Clear day again. We didn't go hunting. Almost out of food and supplies.

Before he left, Ike told a story about finding a walrus out on the rocky top of the Melville Peninsula last year. When the walrus came out onto the ice, it closed behind him. So, the walrus traveled 200 miles to the other side of the Peninsula. Funny, never thought that I would relate to a walrus, but I know how out of place he felt.

The moon tonight is almost full. It's stunning. I put binoculars on it and could see the crater edges. It's so clear.

Polar bear tracks (left), another delectable meal (center) and effects of the cold (right).

Bear tracks are the only sign of hope in what can quickly become a hopeless quest in a brutal, spartan wilderness.

March 18 - The wind picked up today, gusting to 30 mph or more. It was nasty, but we finally struck camp and moved on.

Had an unbelievable experience today. We were on the dogsled when we hit a fresh set of sow and cub tracks. As we looked at the tracks, the dogs went nuts. Off to one side, only 400 yards away, the sow and cub were sniffing seal holes. On the other side, only a few yards away, a second tiny cub headed for the dogs! James handled the dogs, and I picked up the cub and took it to the other side of the sled. We snapped a couple of pictures and sent the cub on its way back to its mother. Last I saw, they were all sniffing seal holes. It was wild.

We just heard that one of the two snow machines, on its way to re-supply us, broke down. We are going to drink the last bit of coffee that we have. Who knows what will happen tomorrow?

March 19 - Ike made it to us late last night with only a small portion of the re-supply and two extra sled dogs to augment the pathetic creatures that we've been using. I believe that they are starting to suffer beyond the call of duty; at least one is on its last legs. For me, it's difficult to watch. I have to force myself to remember that the rules of existence are different here.

We're not going anywhere today. Ike and Daniel are attempting to fix their badly beaten snow machines.

March 20 - The wind has let up. Ike left for Hall Beach. He's left us with one tank of gas in the snow machine and 5 extra gallons in a jerry can; basically another half-tank of gas. Now we'll have to get re-supplied again, barely two days after Ike brought us the last re-supply.

I doubt that James is going to take his dogs anywhere. They've nearly had it. Even with the two new dogs, the team is dragging poorly. I think that James and Daniel are getting awfully tired of this, and that makes three of us.

March 21 - The tent is rattling and shaking, and we are obviously in the middle of a blizzard, so I guess that there won't be any hunting today.

It's around noon, and the blizzard is getting worse. I can barely see the dogs, though they're only 30 or 40 feet from the tent. The tent is taking a pounding as the wind hammers on it. I'm not sure how hard the wind's blowing, but it has got to be 40 mph. It's deafening.

March 22 - It is about 9:30 a.m. We're having eggs in a bag this morning. They keep eggs up here by cracking them into a Zip-top bag. Then they let them freeze. To prepare them, you simply dump them into the frying pan. Everything freezes up here, everything. I was a little colder last night in my sleeping bag; it's getting damp. It's not blizzarding this morning, but it's bad. Still snowing, white-out conditions. We're not going hunting today.

March 23 - This is the 21st day on the ice and the 23rd day of the trip. James is pretty well done. We got our re-supply late this evening. I'm afraid that it's too little, too late. Before our re-supply, we met up with another dog musher out on the ice—our first contact with another human! He killed a small bear yesterday and gave us some ribs. We boiled them right then and there and ate them. Good, but they left a bitter taste in my mouth. I've spent a lifetime dreaming about tasting my own polar bear!

March 24 - It's over. I think that we did our best under the circumstances. With luck it would have been over way back on March 7, when that big bear walked into camp while James and I were a mile away.

Daniel and I want to spend the next few days hunting our way back south, but James won't go on. He can't. He's going home. He's already loading the sled. He's not even taking the tent; he's going to make an igloo every night until he gets back to Hall Beach in four days or so. Hopefully, the dogs will make it. Daniel will pull me back on the komitick.

March 25 - It's 1 a.m., and Daniel and I just got back to Hall Beach after a grueling 12-hour ride. That's it. It's over. I didn't get a polar bear. The worst thing is that I have to go back out into that forsaken place and try again. ❖

Triumphant Return

On May 4, five weeks later, Jim returned to Hall Beach and teamed up again with James and Daniel. On day two of the hunt, Jim killed a muzzleloading world record, 17-year-old boar polar bear.

❖ A Tribute to Him ❖

By David Baty

Easy. Don't move. Not in full strut. Just a single cluck. These words filtered through my mind as I peered at the approaching gobbler. Hidden between two red cedar trees in the Ozark Mountains, I was watching the tom strut and boom his way across the fescue field toward my position. I was spending my first turkey season without my father, but his words continued to guide me. I knew that if I heeded his advice, my chances of succeeding this year were better than not.

My father was reared in the heart of the Ozark Mountains during the Great Depression and saw many of the lean years that accompanied that time. He left Missouri to pursue a career in the oil field, but never gave up the hope of returning to the oak-covered hills of his youth. Over the years, he purchased a farm on a considerable tract of land in the Ozarks, and upon retirement, moved there. He raised cattle on the grassy meadows that were interspersed among the wooded hillsides. His true ambition was to make a living and preserve the native hunting that existed in these hills. Neighbors continued to clear the timber from their property, thus destroying habitat that guaranteed the survival of the wild turkey. Undaunted, Dad always maintained that the wildlife was just as much a part of living as was making money, and there wasn't any way that he would destroy the bedroom of the deer, squirrels and turkeys.

I spent as much time with my dad in the woods as possible, learning. He taught me the reasons for building a pond a certain way to provide year-round water for the cattle without eliminating habitat for fish or destroying land from overflow. He emphasized the need for letting certain types of brush overgrow to allow the rabbits and quail to multiply. He never drove across an uncut hay field for fear of destroying the clutch of a nesting hen turkey. He lived for the time when he could hunt a crusty, old buck or chase after his dogs to corner a coyote. He knew that without taking care to preserve the wildlife, there would be an emptiness within him that money could not fill.

My father was known throughout the area as one of the finest hunters around. He always seemed to kill a turkey, even when there were supposedly none to be found. Venison was always plentiful at the dinner table, and a plate of squirrel gravy and biscuits could be found on most mornings. Dad always told me that he had learned from one of the best.

I have spent many years in college and have been successful in making a good living, but my best education came from the days afield with the man who learned from one of the best. During one of the last years that I hunted with my father, I learned that without patience, nothing will come. We left the house early on that April morning to make the uphill mile walk to a place where we had roosted some turkeys. It was a typical overcast spring morning with a threat of thunderstorms and rain. As we approached the ridge where we had put the old gobbler to bed, lightning flashed in the south and the accompanying thunder brought a "shock" gobble from the tom. Dad quietly eased into a brush pile near the edge of the narrow meadow that separated one ridge from the other. He motioned for me to do the same. As dawn began to break and the distant thunder continued, two other gobblers joined the early morning ritual of answering tree yelps from the roosting hens. The looming rain made its appearance in the form of steady drizzle, and before long the dripping moisture from the trees and brush pile made hearing the flydown impossible. A low-lying mist also reduced visibility of the field to near zero.

Dad used his favorite quote to describe the situation: "There are more ways to not kill a turkey." He used this statement to describe his feelings when something like the weather or a pack of running dogs interfered with his spring ritual. I remember another time that this saying proved true. We were working a gobbler at about 75 yards when the tom suddenly quieted himself and slipped off in the opposite direction. Neither of us had flinched. Peering through the timber, I suddenly came face to face with a female coyote at 10 yards. She, too, was looking for the company of a hen turkey.

After sitting there for nearly an hour, the mist began to lift and, of course, the gobbler was in the field with a harem of hens, already vying for their attention. No amount of seductive calling would entice that old tom away from his undertaking. Tiring of this nonsense and hearing a gobble in the opposite direction, I whispered to Dad that I was going after the other bird. He nodded and smiled. I slipped away and pursued a folly of my own. Two hours later, after coming to a fence that I didn't have permission to cross, I returned to the hillside above the narrow meadow holding the turkeys. Through the timber, I was able to see my father, who was still in the exact position where I had left him. I decided to watch the foray unfolding below me. The gobbler was at the far

edge of the field and the hens were no longer visible. I heard Dad's wing-bone call emit a contented cluck and the resounding answer of the gobbler immediately followed. Strutting and spitting, that old tom made a bee-line for the brush pile with a throaty gobble almost every other step. At about 30 yards from the concealing deadfall, the gobbler stuck his neck out and fell to the blast from Dad's old Winchester shotgun. When I got to the field, my father once again just smiled. It was unbelievable to me that he had remained in that pile of wet logs and multiflora rose brambles for nearly three hours without moving. It was clear that he had surpassed "one of the best" to become "the best," and even more gratifying to me was that I knew him.

As I focused on and diligently heeded these words of wisdom that penetrated my subconscious mind, the old gobbler hung up in the middle of the grassy pasture. He was intent on displaying his courtship ritual for me and expected that any hen worth attending would succumb to his fanfare. As instructed, I didn't move a visible muscle. After a lingering 10 minutes, the tom decided that he had had enough and moved off in the opposite direction. A single cluck from my diaphragm call, directed by my inner thoughts and forced out of my mouth, spun that gobbler on a dime and brought him to within 25 yards. One more time, that old Winchester shotgun boomed across the hills, and a bearded majesty became a feast to be cherished.

As I made my way to the truck, I tried to think of a way to pay tribute to my father for his guidance and wisdom and show the proper respect due to the "the best." Among the red cedars and jack pines of the Ozark Mountains is a small country cemetery where we laid my father to rest. Rather than flowers on his grave, you will find three big wing feathers and two tail feathers of his favorite wild bird. ❖

What's a Nice Girl Like You Doing in a Bog Like This

By Barbara Leibell

It's the fourth evening of my moose hunt in Newfoundland. I am sitting on a knoll amidst a sea of dead fir, alone, overlooking a desolate bog, an icy wind hissing bitterly in my ear. High on a gnarled branch, a crow caws, warning me to be alert, that something is awry. But the cold and the endless days of futile hunting have numbed me, and the crow is like the boy who cried wolf. Nothing is moving to the naked eye except shadows that masquerade as moose. So I lean back and listen: The only other sound is that of branches cracking faintly underfoot—my guide, Art Regular, scouting the woods.

I'm not expecting any moose to show up tonight. It's as if the elusive creatures are deliberately avoiding me since I missed a cow at this same bog two days ago. The memory tortures me as I grip my rifle and huddle to keep warm. As much as I try to think of comforting details to stave off the agonizing remembrance—my two sons, my house in Miami Beach, my butterfly garden—I can't shake it off ...

"I can't find her in my scope!" I screamed at Art when the cow suddenly appeared out of a thicket of trees. (The day before the encounter, I'd fallen hard with my rifle, knocking the scope out of alignment. But inexperience and excitement prevented me from realizing this.) Panicked, I fired two hurried shots. The cow ran, then stopped abruptly as if recognizing my inability and gave me another chance. She cocked her head comically, seeming to say, "It's your move." But I was utterly frozen, and she trotted impatiently back into the forest, shaking her head.

Since that day, I haven't seen another moose. I am beginning to take it as a sign that Somebody Up There doesn't want me to hunt. Tonight, sitting at the same bog, with nothing to lean my back against, which aches from marching through miles of mud, water, branches and brambles that constantly trip me, the question haunts me: Why, why, why am I here?

Backtracking

The decision to hunt was so out of character for me—a Jewish screenwriter and mother—that everyone had a theory for why I was doing it. My mother: I'm angry at my husband and taking it out on the moose. My father: I am reliving his African dreams when he shot a marauding hippo in 1957 in Nigeria. A psychiatrist friend: I'm suffering from temporary obsessive compulsive disorder. My husband: "You want to do WHAT?"

Which is exactly what my father said when I flew off to India 20 years ago to meditate for hours each day, searching for the divine peace that lies behind the mental noise. What he didn't count on was that I'd return a strict vegetarian. It was simply bad karma to kill in order to eat. But the body doesn't always listen to the head, and mine, in particular, protested fiercely against such spiritual logic, hungering for chicken soup and pastrami on rye. Finally, I gave in for health reasons, though my heart never completely accepted that a living thing had to perish so that I could endure.

Then it was my turn to have two sons and learn that young boys don't always comply with one's ideas of how things should be. The issue was guns. I hated the things, feared them, wished that they didn't exist—even toy guns. I pleaded with another mother: Was there no peaceful solution to my boys' natural urge to shoot at things? Finally, the family discovered archery, and the gun issue seemed resolved; that is until my husband discovered bowhunting on the Internet and wanted to try it out on a bear in Newfoundland.

"You want to do WHAT?" I cried in horror.

But he'd made up his mind. The only way I could save the situation was to go along and pray for the bear.

Big moose pulled the author back to Newfoundland for a hunt.

Thank heavens that the place he picked for the hunt, the Ocean Side Country Lodge in Point Leamington, owned by Hazen and Diane Chippett and Ray Saunders, soothed my soul and made me temporarily forget about hunting.

Facing east on Notre Dame Bay, the clear Atlantic waters lapped up on a stony shore, hugged by two wild ridges of ancient rocks and trees. Out the lodge's window, salmon vaulted out of the sea, returning to the Western Arm River, just down the road. In Hazen's boat, we sidled up to a spectacular iceberg, blinding white as angel's wings, and Minke whales, diving to chase a school of fish.

But the gentle dream ended when my husband and another hunter, Bob, marched out the door, gun and bow in hand, gripped by the ubiquitous delirium of the hunter, fever-headed to find their prey. Now I had two bears to pray for. Did God listen? Bob took a 450-pound bruin the third day. I marveled, even as I grieved, at being this close to him, smelling the wilderness steaming off his fur. When Bob said that he was taking the meat home, the bear's death became acceptable, though I never expected a distinguished Vermont

lawyer to eat bear meat.

"Spring bear, lovely tasting," declared Meeta, the cook at Ocean Side's sister lodge, recounting the other critters that she's stewed up: beaver, seal, rabbit, grouse, otter. "And elk and caribou," said Sarah, a 50-something businesswoman who'd come to check out moose hunting in the fall, adding to her freezers of wild game back in Tampa, Florida.

I stared at them in urban abhorrence. Who were these people, the Beverly Hillbillies? Sarah must have discerned my expression and finally explained that she and her husband also enjoyed wild game because it's low-fat and drug-free. And then, she said, there was this special connection to the animal.

Until now, my only experience with hunters had happened years ago when a friend's brother packed his truck with drunken men to shoot wild pigs in an orange grove in northern Florida. I was disgusted. But Sarah and Barbara, a Pennsylvania grandmother, also staying at Ocean Side who, while fearlessly sitting on a rock had shot a bear as he walked by at 20 yards, shattered my stereotype. I wished that I had even a fraction of their courage. But then, hunting meant guns, and guns were not a part of my history like they are with boys. You can't kill a bear with a Barbie doll.

Still, I was curious about the taste of wild game. Diane graciously roasted some moose, and my kids ate it with gusto—and so did I, much to my surprise. Then, days later, I bought a postcard of a moose crossing a road over a lavender sunset, and I dreamed that I followed him across the threshold to a place where I felt no fear. The next morning while trout fishing, Art regaled me with tales of his hunts, and I was once again infected with dreams of moose, until they imploded, and I heard myself blurt out to Hazen, "I want to go moose hunting!"

"You want to do WHAT?" my husband cried in shock. "For the meat," I stumbled. Hazen, seeing that I was in trouble, stepped in. "My duckie, our women hunters have been 100 percent successful. I know you can do it if y'want."

On the Path

That was all the confidence that I needed. Back in

Miami, I bought a .270 Win. rifle, just like Sarah's, recalling her courage when my mouth went dry and my hands trembled as I loaded a cartridge into the chamber. I pulled the trigger, and the butt smashed into my shoulder like a jackhammer. But I'd shot it! Nineteen more cartridges—printed within a hair of each other in the bull's eye at 100 yards. My husband was humbled. A Haitian-born corrections officer who'd helped me sight-in the rifle said, "What do you do for a living? Crash cars?"

I smiled and went back to the store for more cartridges. Near the gun counter, I picked up a video titled, "The Sacred Hunt: Hunting as a Sacred Path," by Randall L. Eaton, Ph.D. And my journey as a hunter was forever changed.

The gist of the video is that the biggest reason why ancient hunters hunted was to have an experience of Divine Connection with the Sacred.

My Sacred Hunt

And I recall now why I've come here, as I sit at this primeval bog tonight, aching and freezing, waiting for a moose. In the distance, I hear Art calling softly: "Mawwww. Mawww." I gawk at the sky as it turns tangerine and lavender, like the sunset on the postcard of the moose crossing the road.

Then, like a spirit, a bull moose walks out of the woods about 400 yards away.

My heart stops. Then races.

I watch him through my scope. He is breathtaking, magnificent, standing between two trees. My mind is screaming: Should I shoot? Too far. What if he goes back into the woods? My God, I'm alone! Art, I need you to talk me through this! But Art is off calling the bull out. I know that I need to calm down.

I slow my breath, controlling it, meditating with my eyes open, focusing on the moose like a mantra. Stillness lies behind the mental noise, I remember, using a technique that I learned from a meditation master: Watching one's thoughts instead of becoming entangled in them. Letting them come and go, without hooking into their frantic emotion. Breathing, breathing ... my heart and mind grow calm. Everything is still. I am only seeing the moose.

The author, taking careful aim at a moose across the bog.

I glance to my right. Art is now standing at the edge of the bog, smiling. The moose has stopped 200 yards away, his nose in the air, catching my scent, offering himself for a fraction of a second. It's my decision to cross the road with him. I hear the silence shatter, the explosion echoing through the hills. Then, like a curtain going down at the end of a play, the sun descends over the horizon, blinding me. I do not see the bull when he falls into the woods.

Art runs toward me on the knoll like a proud father. I put my head on my rifle and weep.

Back in Miami, the tears still fall as my family eats moose steak, and we thank the Spirit that feeds us. Then, I watch the boys hunt lizards in the yard, honoring the urges that they've inherited from their ancient grandfathers. I call Randall to tell him my story. His arrows always shoot from the heart. "Hunting is like the love between a man and a woman," he says. "You don't stop to analyze it, but fall into the love of it."

I have fallen inescapably into the ubiquitous delirium of the hunter, and I will return in the autumn to Newfoundland with sacred dreams of moose. ❖

❖ Elk Hunting for Two ❖

By Mark Kayser

As hunters, we try to uphold the image of being rugged, tough individuals. How tough would you be if you were five months pregnant and on a rigorous mountain elk hunt?

I'd bet that most men wouldn't pass muster. Being pregnant demands a lot from a woman's body. Trust me, I've been through it twice. Well, my wife, Sharon, has been through it, and I wouldn't want to be in her pregnant shoes even for the chance at a Boone and Crockett Club critter.

Jodi Madison, a five-months pregnant mother from Mobridge, South Dakota, faced up to the challenge after she and her husband, Shawn, drew coveted Black Hills elk tags. Not only did she face morning sickness and fatigue from nourishing a developing baby, but she also had to surmount physical exhaustion, mountain altitudes and bone-chilling temperatures.

Drawing the elk tags together was especially exciting for Shawn because he grew up in the hills and knows its big bull history. Aggressive campaigns to deter poaching, a changing forest environment suited for elk and conservative elk management have created a laudable elk herd. Black Hills hunters enjoy some of the highest success rates in the nation for public land hunting, with bulls grossing more than 380 inches showing up every year.

Shawn, a conservation officer with the South Dakota Department of Game, Fish and Parks, scheduled his busy fall to be with Jodi on the opening day of elk season. Chris Yeoman, a longtime friend who lives in New Mexico and guides on the famed Vermejo Park Ranch, also promised to meet them for the hunt.

Opening morning was quiet, even though they had seen a 5-point bull in the area the evening before. Deer sightings and an encounter with a herd of bighorn sheep made the morning hunt memorable, but a five-hour hike and morning sickness exhausted Jodi. She opted to rest at the truck while Chris and Shawn scouted a new area.

Jodi's afternoon nap was awakened by a bull's bugle. Unbeknownst to her, Shawn and Chris worked that bull only to have it escape, but not without seeing enough antler to realize its monstrous proportions.

Jodi felt that she needed to return to Mobridge to recuperate after four days of hunting and little action. Chris and Shawn decided to continue hunting. Moving into a new area saturated with rubs changed their luck. During the next afternoon, elk appeared like trick-or-treaters on Halloween. Shawn passed on five different 6-point bulls, including one in the 300-inch range, as he and Chris targeted a herd bull. The aggressive bull succumbed to a cow call just before dark, offering Shawn a 100-yard shot. Tines measuring 19 inches combined with a 50-inch spread gave the bull a score of 340 inches and Shawn enough confidence to urge Jodi to return.

Jodi's father drove her the three hours back to the Black Hills to hunt the new area. The next afternoon, the group sneaked into Shawn's honey hole, but the trick-or-treaters played a trick and couldn't be heard.

The hunters returned before dawn the next morning and passed the drainage where they saw the monster bull on opening day. Moonlight revealed elk scattered across the meadow.

Shawn and Jodi hiked through the darkness to a dis-tant ridge in an attempt to ambush the elk leaving the meadow at daylight. The approaching bull's bugles filtering through the trees had Shawn's heart pounding, but Jodi remained calm, even though she could barely feel her toes from the October chill.

When the monster bull appeared through an opening, Jodi didn't need a nudge to tell her to shoot, and the bull humped at the rifle's report. A second shot sent the bull staggering over the ridge. The hunters scrambled over the hill and were greeted by a massive 7x6 bull that gross scored 382 inches.

With both the hunt and the pregnancy behind Jodi, she now has two trophies to add to the family's South Dakota home. It goes without saying that the more memorable one is named Grace, who joins her sister Shawna and brother Jaden. ❖

Jodi Madison with her massive 7x6 bull elk that measured 382 inches.

❖ LAST TRIP TO HIDEOUT FOLD ❖

By Bill Sansom

Every hunter dreams of a special place; one that is his alone, an untouched oasis where a lifetime of memories await. Hideout Fold was a reality, beckoning the old man to answer its call for one final memory.

The bull elk shook his massive head and snorted. Puffs of vapor churned out of his nostrils and drifted up and back through the heavy tines of his wide 6-point rack. The sound came again, faint and far away. He started to move, angling downslope through a patch of young fir trees. Gusts of chilling wind riffled the long black hair of his neck mane and creaked a limbless and leaning lodgepole pine against another. The aging bull knew that sound well. He also knew the distant sound—one that meant danger. During the past two months, he'd been constantly on the move; fighting, breeding. A painful shoulder wound—the price for answering a bowhunter's bugle—had weakened him further. Although the bull managed to dislodge the razor-sharp broadhead, the wound was still sore and the nagging pain made him wary of the distant call.

The bull slipped into a heavy stand of lodgepole and turned onto a thread-thin strand of a game trail, which led into a steep-walled draw that held a seeping trickle of water. His hooves cracked the ice crust on the mossy rocks as he stepped across the stream. He pushed his way through a tangle of snowy brush, his ivory-tipped tines brushing against the bent limbs, showering him with snow. The draw widened a half-mile below and joined a larger gulch created by a bigger stream.

A spray of sparks burst out of the chimney of the larger of two brown canvas tents set off the edge of a road. A battered red pickup, with a horse trailer behind, was parked next to the tents. One orange-clad figure chopped wood, another threw hay to four horses that stood in a rope corral. The wind carried the smoke and other odors to the bull, and he whirled in his tracks and trotted back the way that he had come. He stopped where the trees broke and stood there for several minutes studying the two-acre opening. Then he ghosted around the clearing,

just inside the trees and picked up the game trail again on the far side.

Western Montana's mountains are grouped into several major ranges, partitioned into various drainages and smaller tributaries. Individual mountains have descriptive titles, and ridges and gulches on these mountains are also named. You can pick up a map and memorize the names, but you must hunt the mountain to really know it—to know about the room-sized feeder openings and pine-cloaked parks. You must be a student of the mountain to learn about the finger ridges, the elk wallows, the thin game trails. You could hunt a mountain for years and never cover all of it. There will still be a place, maybe only a few acres in size, that will remain undiscovered and unhunted.

The old bull headed for just such a place. It was no more than a slight fold on a steep, flat-faced, fir-blanketed mountainside. An ancient overgrown logging skid trail bisected one edge of the fold. The crease held a spring that bubbled and seeped for a few dozen yards before sinking back underground. A couple of small openings dotted the side of the wrinkle that faced the mountainside.

The old bull couldn't have reasoned that this particular spot was not well-known to the tide of hunters who would be surging across the more popular ridges in just a few hours. Wildlife biologists argue that elk can't reason, that they're incapable of putting together a chain of thoughts. They call it instinct or luck. But the old bull knew this place, this hideout, and he knew that it was quiet here; calm, safe. He couldn't have known about the old man who had last hunted there the fall before the bull was born.

The old man shrugged deeper into his mackinaw coat. His pale blue eyes scanned the cloud-shrouded ridges.

He sensed the coming snow in the crispness of the air, and in the way that his shepherd dog was lying curled up out of the wind. He bent over and picked up a couple extra pieces of the tamarack that he had split and piled them on top of the load in his wheelbarrow.

His son, with his young family in tow, turned into the driveway for their nightly visit to check the progress of the carpenters who were building them a new house just across the street. The old man waved a hello to his daughter-in-law and the two kids, as they hopped out of the pickup and scampered off in the direction of the new house. His son sauntered over to the woodpile.

"Looks like a storm's brewing," he said as he reached out and petted the dog that had trotted up to greet him.

"Yep, we'll probably have a couple inches by morning. Got the tea water hot. Here, push this wheelbarrow in for me. You goin' out tomorrow?"

"Can't in the morning—gotta work—maybe in the evening. I'm off Sunday, wanna go out?" The old-timer hadn't hunted much for several years. His wind had been bothering him lately—doctor said that it was emphysema—and the mountains were getting too steep for him.

The son pushed the wheelbarrow into the house and unloaded the wood beside the crackling cookstove. Half hoping that it would goad his son into skipping work the next morning, the old man said, "I might go out in the morning if I'm feeling okay." He knew that his son still looked forward to their infrequent hunts together. "Why don't you skip a shift? We could hunt Prospector Ridge."

"Naw, we'll be plenty busy tomorrow. Let's go out Sunday."

"Sunday you'll be dragging mine out," the old hunter answered. He could feel a twinge of enthusiasm building somewhere deep inside. Maybe he really would go out in the morning.

The kitchen door burst open and his grandkids spilled into the room. "Hi Grandpa!" the boy shouted. "Going huntin' tomorrow? Dad's taking me out tomorrow night. We're gonna get an elk an' a deer. I get to take my BB gun."

The old man glanced at his son. The tradition passes on, he thought. "You chatter worse'n a squirrel," the old man scolded as he tousled the boy's hair. He sat down and picked up the little girl, setting her on his knee. It

will be good to have them next door, close by, he thought.

After they left, the old man poked another stick of wood into the cookstove. He poured another cup of tea and watched it steam awhile. Then he slid open a cupboard drawer and removed a bone-handled hunting knife. He rummaged around, gathering his gear, opening a tattered box of .30-30 shells, slipping a worn and rust-pocked Winchester modified 94 out of its doeskin scabbard. Preparations completed, he opened the kitchen door, leaned against the jamb and gazed into the fading daylight. He felt good, better than he had for a long time, maybe even a little excited.

Snow started to fall out of the darkening sky, small flakes already skiffing on the fence posts and roofs. His eyes shifted again to the misty ridgetops. The gray clouds rushed down their flanks. The old hunter's eyebrows furrowed momentarily, then a smile spread across his face. Maybe I can make it up there again, he thought, maybe one last time. He hadn't been there for years, though he could almost see it from his kitchen doorway. It wasn't much of a spot, really. It was no more than a slight fold on a steep, flat-faced, fir-covered mountainside. An ancient overgrown skid trail traced a faint seam in the canopy down one side of the fold.

It was still two hours until dawn. He clicked five rounds into the rifle's magazine and quietly stepped into the timber. He paused to catch his wind, wondering if he could make the climb—and if there would be anything there when he did. He turned and looked back at his truck, and with a shrug, he decided that it didn't matter one way or the other.

The bull's senses tuned to a heightened state. He could hear the traffic whizzing along on the paved road in the valley below him. Standing, he could've seen the headlights of the vehicles churning up the mountain road three-quarters of a mile west of him, in the predawn blackness. The whole area buzzed with activity, hunters jockeying for their spots. Soon, the main ridges and forest service trails would be blinking with flashlight beams shining through the dark timber.

The skid trail steepened. The old man moved a few more yards, then stopped until the thumping eased in his chest. He fought back an urge to turn around. Go back to the cozy house. Have a cup of tea. Read another paperback. Stoke the fire, take a nap and dream about the long gone days of beaver-dammed drainages teeming with cutthroat trout, the sudden focus of a fresh grizzly track, a bull elk pivoting his gnarled horns, threading his way through a thick stand of lodgepole.

The first gray shades of dawn began filtering across the hillsides and seeping over the eastern ridges. He slowly worked his way upward toward the fold.

The bull was up again. He shifted his position closer to the crest of the fold, where the prevailing draft would carry the scent of anything approaching from below.

The old hunter reached the end of the skid trail and side-hilled around to his left. He moved with a slow deliberate silence—crossing the spring where it sank back into the ground—and took up a position where he could watch the openings across the draw. He could just begin to make out shapes at 20 yards, then 40. He heard a faint staccato of shots echo from a far-off ridge. Someone had gotten lucky, or almost, doing it the easy way—from a road.

At the sound of the shots, the old bull went on full alert. He was bedded again, but his head was erect and his ears twitched forward, then back. His nose tested the trickle of air rising up from the bottoms. Then he sensed a change in the wind and stood up to reposition himself.

It was dawn. The old hunter's first study of the openings revealed no animals. He felt the chill creeping inside his coat, and his toes were stinging with cold. Maybe he would start a small fire in a little while, but first he would make another bush-by-bush inspection of the openings. His eyes scanned the clearings, studying them a section at a time. There! Near the top. An antler tip. No—wait a minute—yep, there he is! The bull's shape focused out of the surrounding brush. He was quartering away, standing one jump from the edge of the fold—and escape.

The bull turned slightly, presenting a broadside shot. Already, automatically, the front bead of the rifle sight had settled in the notch of the rear buckhorn sight, and both were aligned perfectly with a spot an inch behind the bull's right front shoulder. The bull lowered his head to nip at the brush.

Sights still on the bull, the old hunter eased off the pressure that he was beginning to apply to the trigger.

How many hunts had there been? How many elk? Did he need this one? What would it bring? One more hunting story. He had little taste for meat anymore, and did he really need more antlers joining the weather-bleached ones on the wall of his woodshed? Another coughing spasm rose up in the old man's chest. He tried to muffle it in the sleeve of his coat, shoulders shaking.

The bull whirled, swapping ends in his tracks, eyes searching for the source of the stifled sound. He looked toward the trail at the head of the spring and trotted a few steps in that direction.

The old hunter instantly noted the bull's limping gait. When the elk stopped broadside at 30 yards, he quickly sized up the bull's general condition. He appeared gaunt, hurt. A blast of freezing wind whipped around the old man. He knew that it was the beginning of a long cold winter, with deep snow. He raised his .30-30 again. The sights snugged in behind the bull's left shoulder, then traveled up along his neck to a spot behind his eye and below the base of his left antler. His trigger finger squeezed, and the cocked hammer fell. ❖

Epilogue

I packed out his elk the next morning. It hadn't snowed more than a few inches since the morning before. I was curious about where the bull came from, so I backtracked him and discovered this story. When I returned to the fold, I studied it carefully. I noticed new and old scrapes on the lodgepole and fir. The browse showed evidence of use over the years. I even found a chunk of squirrel-chewed elk antler in a thicket. My findings confirmed what my dad had always told me: "The smart, old bulls hide when opening day comes, so don't go following all those other hunters. Go where no one else wants to go—except the elk." My dad took his last hunt to Hideout Fold in 1976. His ashes were scattered there in 1993.

The fold is still there, untouched, unhunted. The wind whispers through the fir trees, old bulls still drink from the trickle where it pools before sinking into the ground. I go there once a year, on opening day, for the elk—and the memories.

DEER CRAZY

Hunters go nuts for deer. As a matter of fact, we're downright crazy. Deer crazy.

Guns, bows and muzzleloaders. Cartridges, slugs, arrows and loads. Scouting, sighting-in, shooting practice. Camouflage, blaze orange, boots and gloves. Treestands, ground blinds, decoys and scents. Hours and hours waiting on stand, or sneaking through the woods. How much money and time do we devote to this craziness?

But all the hours, all the days, all the preparation, all the dreams, all the longing … when everything finally comes together again and the buck or doe is down and the total bill in dollars and hours is tallied … well, nobody ever tallies that kind of stuff.

Because we're crazy for deer. And it's all worth it!

❖ THE SCIENCE OF SCENT CONTROL ❖

By Gary Clancy

As part of my research for this article, I thumbed through the most recent Cabela's Master Catalog and counted 30 items, ranging from complete camouflage suits to backpacks, featuring a layer of activated carbon (AC) for controlling human odor. I thought to myself, "We've come a long way, baby!"

Back during the fall of 1991, I was one of a handful of hunters field testing a new product called Scent-Lok. At the time, Scent-Lok suits were only available in one style—solid green pull-on pants with a pullover top. Because those early suits had a harsh, noisy finish and were not available in camouflage, I wore my suit as a layer between my underwear and outer layer.

During those early years, I took a lot of guff from fellow hunters for wearing that funny green suit. Many who saw me wearing it wrote Scent-Lok off as another in a long line of gimmicks designed to accomplish nothing more than separating a hunter from his dollars.

I'll admit that I was skeptical, too, when Greg Sesselmann, the man who started this whole AC thing, first asked me to give his green suit a try. But then I had been skeptical of odor-reducing sprays and powders when they first came out, too, and I had learned through using them that those products helped in the battle to beat the whitetail's nose.

"Maybe this kid from Michigan is onto something," I thought. Turns out that he was—big time!

Today, as evidenced by the number of products featuring AC technology in that Cabela's catalog, it is obvious that many of those skeptics have become believers. The long list of manufacturers who make scent-control products for big game hunters includes: Browning, Cabela's, Whitewater Outdoors, Bass Pro Shops, Fieldline, Double Bull Blinds, Hidden Wolf, Johnson Garments, LaCrosse, Wolverine Boots and a growing number of others that I do not have room to mention. These manufacturers offer their wares because AC works.

Here's How It Works

The AC used in hunting products is made from coal, wood and coconut shells. The raw material that is used has a large influence on the performance of activated carbon. The raw material is heated at more than 900°C creating the activated carbon that adsorbs gas and solid scent molecules. The adsorption takes place when the molecules bond themselves to the surface of the carbon. My dictionary defines adsorption as: The adhesion, in an extremely thin layer, of the molecules of gases of dissolved substances, or of liquids, to the surfaces of solid bodies with which they are in contact—distinguished from absorption.

The three major players in the AC industry—Scent-Lok; W.L. Gore and Associates, which manufactures Supprescent; and Robinson Labs Scent Blocker—use different methods of holding the AC in place between layers of fabric, but the AC used is similar and does its job in a similar manner. The key to scent control is having enough carbon surface area to adsorb odors over a long period of time. AC has countless cracks and crevices where the scent molecules are attracted and concentrated. In fact, 5 grams of activated carbon can have the surface area of a football field. This means that a large concentration of scent particles can be adsorbed before the reactivation process is necessary.

AC was not invented for you and me to be able to more effectively hunt white-tailed deer or other big game animals that rely upon a keen sense of smell. It has been widely used by industry and the military for decades to perform a wide variety of functions. Sesselmann just happened to have the foresight to see the application for AC in the hunting industry.

Reactivation of AC

There will come a time when the AC in your hunting clothes will have done all that it can do. When all of the surface area of the AC is already holding and grasping

Activated carbon (AC) clothing can make a real difference in controlling human odor … which means more and closer encounters with deer.

the stuff that makes you and me stink, those odors will pass through to the air outside our clothing and once again we will find ourselves busted by the incredible nose of some big game animal. Luckily, instead of throwing the garment away and being forced to purchase a new one, there is a reactivation process that we can use to help the AC shed some of its load, thus opening up surface area for the capture of more smelly stuff. You can reactivate your AC garment by tossing it in a clothes dryer for 45 minutes on the high heat mode. Take it out and presto, you're back in business.

How often you should reactivate your AC clothing depends upon a number of factors, including outside air temperatures, which will determine how much you sweat inside your suit and how bad you stink. Hey, all of us have body odor, but some have it worse than others. I toss my AC suit into the dryer after every 30 hours of wear. That timetable has worked for me and

for those who have adopted my schedule. If that is not often enough for you, the deer will let you know in a hurry that you need to reactivate your AC garment more frequently.

You can wash an AC garment without harming it, but since washing does nothing to reactivate or "cleanse" the AC, I wash my newer AC outerwear garments only when they are so covered with blood or mud that the original camouflage pattern is impossible to recognize. If I am wearing an AC outer garment, however, I always spray its exterior with an odor-neutralizing spray, such as Scent-A-Way or Carbon Blast, just as a precaution in case I have gotten human odor or other foreign odors on the surface.

I store my AC garments in one of those dark green H.S. Scent Safe bags (ordered at www.hunterspec.com) between hunts so that they do not become contaminated with unwanted foreign odors.

Not a Cure-All

Like thousands of other serious big game hunters, I believe in the effectiveness of AC garments. I've probably been wearing them longer than anyone reading this article, and since that first season, I have recognized that AC is a huge weapon in the war against the whitetail's nose. But as good as AC is at doing what it does, it is not a cure-all. If you insist on putting on your AC garment at home and then stopping at the cafe for bacon and eggs, gassing up the truck and maybe having a few cigarettes on the drive to your hunting area, it's not going to shield you from the whitetail's nose. Or if you do not shower with an odor-free soap before your hunt, apply an odorless anti-perspirant or take precautions to ensure that the rest of your clothing is odor free, your AC garment will be hard-pressed to do its job, although even under these less-than-ideal conditions, wearing it will help.

I feel confident in making that statement, because during the second year that I wore Scent-Lok, my elk hunting partner and I drew Arizona elk tags and spent 21 wonderful days scouting and hunting for the big bulls for which that state is justifiably famous. I only had the Scent-Lok liner suit then, so when we went to our evening stands over waterholes, whoever had the worst wind wore the Scent-Lok. Even under elk camp conditions where a shower was an every-fourth-day luxury, time after time, that Scent-Lok liner prevented us from being smelled by elk coming to drink.

But under normal hunting conditions, wearing an AC garment is one step in a series of many that I take to control my human odor. Granted, it might be the biggest step that I've ever taken in that direction, but it's still only one step. A clean body, clean clothing, making use of odor-reducing sprays and powders, and above all, trying to always hunt with the wind in my favor, are other important ingredients to any recipe for successful odor control. ❖

Contain Clothing

Last season, I added a new weapon to my defense arsenal when I began field-testing Contain clothing. Contain is not an activated carbon product, but I have found it to be a great complement to activated carbon clothing. Contain works like this: Triclosan, an anti-bacterial compound commonly used in hand soaps and underarm anti-perspirants, attacks and kills the cell walls of bacteria to prevent them from producing odor. Triclosan is mixed with acetate and then extruded into a fiber. The fiber is then blended with other fibers and woven into the fabric of the cloth. You can wash the garment as often as you like without compromising its effectiveness.

It makes sense to me that if Contain can prevent some or all of the odor molecules from forming in my clothing, then my activated carbon does not have to work as hard and will be even more beneficial. It is my guess that you will be hearing more about Contain during the next few years.

Make scent control a multifaceted affair—from the clothes you put on, to the boots you wear, to what you eat.

❖ WHITETAIL CALLING COLLEGE ❖

By Mark Kayser

College—or the more politically correct term, university—conjures images of library study sessions, fall homecomings and graduation ceremonies. All right, I'll be honest, a few wilder images come to mind, too. But probably my most memorable moments were my wild pursuits of whitetails between classes. Even more exciting was my newfound success in calling whitetails. That was during the late 1980s, but even today, calling bucks continues to give me a college-style rush.

Learning to proficiently call deer takes on a school-like progression. Most hunters master the basics, attaining a high school degree in calling. A few take it a step further, pursuing an advanced degree.

Getting a college degree in whitetail calling requires an intimate knowledge of whitetail ecology, a topographical map-like knowledge of your hunting areas and proficiency in using a variety of deer calls. Get passing grades in these areas, and you'll be on your way to a college degree in whitetail calling. Gain in-the-field experience and you'll pass with flying colors. It's great fun, except for the out-of-state hunting tuition in the form of nonresident hunting licenses, but that's all part of the learning curve.

Whitetail Characteristics

To call whitetails, you have to understand them. You have to be able to read their body language to determine how aggressively you should call. It doesn't pay to hammer on a set of rattling horns to a recently antler-whipped 2½-year-old buck. He's heading for the far side of the county to lick his wounds, and his body language will show his meekness. On the other hand, a 5½-year-old stud sporting 150 inches of antler and walking stiff-legged with bristled neck hairs has the makings for an exciting calling setup.

A whitetail's body language delivers a message that no mime can match. It just takes a bit more experience to be able to read it. Determining whether a buck is in an aggressive or neutral mood makes a world of difference when calling.

Much of what a deer says centers around the head. Eye contact, position of the ears, flared nostrils and erect hair all tell a message. Dominant bucks seldom stare at lesser males in close proximity. Young bucks, on the other hand, will glance at their leaders, while checking their backside for a dominant jab. Determining whether a buck sports dominant characteristics doesn't matter for most hunters, though. Any buck will do. But if you come across a field milling with bucks, it pays to know which one will most likely respond to your calls.

If a buck is casually moving through the woods, the odds are good that he'll respond. Look for telltale signs like sniffing the ground, constant searching, erect tail and tree sparring. A buck exhibiting these actions is a sucker for the call.

If I'm lucky enough to see a buck interacting with other deer, the odds increase of him showing even better signals. When a more dominant buck enters the scene, all whitetail understudies take notice. When bucks come together, one of two things can happen. Either they'll avoid each other or begin a game of intimidation, walking past each other with hair bristled, ears laid back and the whites of their eyes showing. Bucks don't get much more aggressive than this except when they actually fight. And if one buck gets run off, I feel confident that I can usually call in the winner.

If I had to sum up what to look for, it would be confidence. Confidence shows in people and in animals. A mature, dominant whitetail approaches other deer without hesitation. That's the buck to target.

Bucks one level below the local honcho want to act like the big boys, but retreat quickly when confronted. Although I'll call to almost every buck that catches my antler fancy, I don't put much hope in bucks that skirt dominant bucks, refuse to display laid-back ears, keep their hair flat or appear wounded from earlier fights. They probably won't come.

When you're rattling, the big boys are often the ones to come in. A subdominant buck will usually want to avoid another whipping and will be less likely to approach the sound of clashing antlers.

Since many deer herds in North America don't fit the model age-class structure, don't always look for a monster buck to be the dominant animal. The average buck harvested in many states is only 1½ years old. The largest buck that I've shot, a 170-class animal, was the runt of the herd in dominance stature. His antlers out-classed every local buck, but his young body didn't match his ornate headgear. Any 120- or 130-class buck with a mature body pushed him around. I ended his frustrating morning of rutting with one well-placed shot from my Remington .300 Win. Mag.

Reading a whitetail only works when you can see it. To get the most out of calling, you'll have to call blind during the majority of setups. That's where the next course of study comes into play; getting into a whitetail's home undetected.

Whitetail Hideouts

One would think that you'd need a topographical background of an area to know where to best locate whitetails. This is true, but I use topographical information more for entering a whitetail's home. For me, graduating with honors centers around the knowledge of how to approach a calling location. Knowing their home and their calls plays an important role. But they don't mean anything if you don't know how to get into a deer's home undetected.

Finding entrances and alleys into a buck's home range takes some caffeine-enhanced studying like those college all-nighters. Topographical maps, aerial photographs and on-the-ground scouting provide the information needed to crawl into a buck's lair. Look at the area that you plan to hunt and determine the easiest path into the deer's bedroom. Now forget that path and look for an out-of-the-way back door. A buck is going to be watching all obvious entrances. Look for depressions, ridges and other natural features to cover your approach. If no such features exist, use the cover of darkness to get in and out of an area without being detected. Fog is also a blessing from above.

One of my favorite waterway tactics is hiking below the bank of rivers and creeks. The bank hides my form and often funnels my scent down the winding river like the water current. I'll admit, when guiding, I've been given some strange looks when diving off a bank to wade in ice-jammed water or along a frozen river, but my approach always surprises bucks. It's not uncommon to approach within eyesight of unsuspecting deer that have their attention riveted toward a field edge where danger normally arrives in the form of a rumbling pickup.

While guiding clients in Montana last fall, three of us clamored along an icy bank for nearly a half-mile, finally crawling up the bank and into a stand of cottonwoods. We were immediately surrounded by whitetails and mulies. Within an hour, we targeted a dominant buck. His rutting frenzy had him making house calls throughout the woods, visiting all the local ladies. Rattling and grunting grabbed his attention, and within minutes, my client pulled the trigger at 50 steps. Had we approached that buck in a traditional manner, we would have blown the entire group out of the timber.

Whitetail Communication

As a clarification, you won't see me trying to spell out deer noises in text. Why? I've yet to read a noise like "brrrrrump" and know how to make it on my own call. Take the time to talk to an expert, buy a cassette or CD, or rent a video. Hearing the sound firsthand will eliminate your frustration in trying to decipher my interpretation of the sound "brrrrrump."

As in many college curriculums, it seems like the fun courses always come after the brain benders. Why did I need college-level algebra before I could take an introductory course in photography? The same applies to whitetail hunting. First, learn about the quarry, and then analyze their home for the best entrance and calling sites. After passing those courses, it's time to blow on the call and bang on the antlers for some fun.

Calling is probably the least complicated of the three steps, and the way that you call depends on the previous two steps. You need to get close to deer undetected and be able to judge a deer's state of mind to determine which call to use and at what intensity.

There are three main calls that hunters should focus on: buck calls, doe calls and antler rattling. By no means is whitetail communication that simple. Researchers have only begun to understand the many ways that animals communicate, but the average hunter can easily find success by mastering these calls.

Calls vary with the phases of the fall. During early fall, a hunter's calls should mimic frisky, but not overly aggressive, deer activity. Deer at this time of year generally respond out of curiosity, and you don't want to

A variety of manufactured deer calls are available that will imitate vocal and antler noises made by whitetails.

scare them away. Probably the most effective call is the sparring call created with antlers or a rattling box. It attracts bucks like a wrestling match attracts neighborhood kids. They want to see who is the toughest without actually drawing blood. Most clashes that I've witnessed during September consist of pushing, shoving and low-intensity antler clashes. Clicking of antlers works better than an all-out thrashing.

Another curiosity call, or confidence call, is the doe and fawn bleat. Although bucks come to this call during the early season, the reassuring sounds of does and fawns calms a buck and gives him confidence to approach an area. When hunting field edges just inside the woods, this call helps to ease a buck's fears and can increase the appearance of a buck from timber before it's too dark to shoot.

Finally, don't forget to add in a series of grunts while calling during the early fall. Bucks definitely target this call and might run in unexpectedly or just cruise by looking for action. One of my best early-season success stories involved grunting at a buck as it cruised the edge of a hay field with a bachelor group. Upon hearing the calls, the buck charged into the brush like a rut-crazed animal. Unfortunately, my misjudgment of distance sent the arrow winging harmlessly over his back. The missed shot stunk, but the calling experience boosted my confidence off the charts.

When bachelor groups disband, calling can get crazy as bucks compete for dominance and does. During the nutty season, I rely heavily on grunts and antler rattling. That's not to say that bleats won't work, because the doe-in-heat bleat, an extension of the doe and fawn communication bleat, calls bucks readily. Eddie Salter, a Hunter's Specialties pro staffer, gave me a firsthand lesson in this call, and I've been wooing bucks ever since.

After sneaking into a stand or an ideal calling location, I usually begin with a short series of grunts. A buck might be bedded nearby and the loud clashing of antlers can easily shock him into retreat. If nothing appears after five minutes or so, I bang on the antlers. Again, I like to start out soft, building during the second series into an all-out brawl. To my knowledge, there is no right or wrong way to rattle. No two deer fight the same. I believe in whacking trees, thrashing

Include grunting in your calling repertoire.

branches and stomping leaves to create the sounds of two bucks shoving each other around the woods. If the brush is thick, don't worry about body movement. If a buck sees movement and hears the correct sound, he'll often mistake you for the deer. Be sure to intercept the buck before it circles downwind as all bucks do, and especially be aware of other hunters stalking your position.

For added realism, throw in the snort-wheeze call used by bucks prior to a fight. Remember my description of bucks walking parallel to each other? Often, they'll pass each other and exhale viciously in a long hissing sound. This call might be the most dominant vocalization of a whitetail and again needs to be witnessed or demonstrated by an expert to be properly mimicked.

If you still have unused tags going into the late season, use the rut calls. Doing so gives bucks a reason to go looking for a doe coming into heat late. As during the early season though, tone the call back a notch. Remember that bucks just finished a nonstop breeding marathon and although another doe is welcome, they don't always have the lungs or legs for Olympic-style breeding.

Sure, calling doesn't work all the time. What tactic does? But when it does work, the excitement level rises above the shenanigans of any wild college weekend. Okay, almost any. ❖

❖ Treestand Techniques ❖

By Bob Robb

Under many circumstances, hunting from a treestand can be the most effective method of all, especially in areas with relatively high game populations, dense cover and terrain that's too flat to permit much glassing. Successful treestand hunting, however, involves much more than simply buying a stand, randomly picking out a tree and climbing up. It's a chess game, a dynamic process of moves and countermoves; where the hunter selects a tree for his stand, gives it a go and then, based on his observations and changes in prevailing conditions, might choose to move the stand to increase his chances at a high-percentage shot.

IMPROVING YOUR ODDS

Here are some guidelines that will help make you a more successful treestand hunter:

Scout

You must scout to locate areas where animal sign is abundant before choosing a stand site. For white-tailed deer, such areas can include preferred food sources like acorns, corn fields, alfalfa fields and apple trees; active trails and trail junctions; funnels, green field edges and fence lines; scrapes and rubs. Look for fresh deer droppings, tracks and signs of feeding activity like fresh acorn caps, half-chewed corncobs and places where the ends of browse like honeysuckle have been nibbled on.

As a general rule, the best treestand locations for whitetails cover trails leading from food sources to bedding areas in the mornings and are close to preferred food sources in the afternoons.

Hunt Deer Not Trees

The right way to look for a place to hang a treestand is to scout the woods, find hot sign and then set up within good shooting range of that sign. The wrong way is to scout, find hot sign, then look for a nearby tree that will accommodate your treestand. That's like the tail wagging the dog. Never forget that the objective is to get a shot at your quarry. If your stand won't

work in a tree within range of the spot that you know will produce, it's time to reevaluate your hunting technique and your stand.

Watch the Wind

Even if you're 20 feet off the ground, you still have to hunt with the wind in your favor. Setting up so that game will approach upwind or crosswind of your stand and walking to your stand with the wind in your face are important. For example, when hunting a fresh scrape, it's better to set up 30 to 100 yards downwind of the scrape and not right on it. Just how far depends on the terrain and thickness of the brush. A buck usually approaches a scrape on the downwind side to scent-check it before approaching; you don't want him coming in downwind of you.

Cover

Contrary to popular opinion, deer do look up! Erect your stands so that you have as much cover around you as possible so that deer and other game won't spot your movements or your silhouette. You should at least have a backdrop of leaves and branches. Because most trees are bare by late season, place stands in small clumps of trees so that the multiple trunks offer cover. Don't prune away too many branches around your stand and on the ground to create shooting lanes, or game will spot you.

Don't Move

Just because you're elevated and in full camo doesn't mean that game can't spot your movements. They can! Control your fidgeting by bringing a book to read while on stand. You can cut and stick branches in the floor of your stand so that game can't see your feet shuffling. The less you move, the more game you'll see.

Beware of Hollows

If you place your stand in a hollow, you must be aware that deer might be moving on your level on the

adjacent hillsides. This makes it easier for them to spot you. I always erect my stands either in the very bottom of a hollow or the top of the ridge, but never on a hillside.

Stand Height

Choose your stand's height according to conditions. On flat, open ground, 12 feet might be enough. In thickets, 20 to 25 feet up might be necessary. Do what's necessary to achieve the optimum compromise between cover, visibility, scent control and your height comfort level. I prefer stands set about 25 feet up to prevent game from seeing me, and the added height helps keep my scent floating above game.

Be Quiet

Be as quiet as possible when setting up a stand, traveling to and from the stand site and while sitting on stand. Unnatural noise is a red flag to wary game. Secure all stand parts, like chains and exposed metal surfaces, when you're hauling your stand in. Before the season, lubricate squeaky areas to remove creaks and groans. An old piece of carpet cut to fit makes a warm, quiet foot pad. Take a few extra minutes to take care of details and you'll increase your odds of success.

Minimize Your Gear

Some hunters aren't comfortable unless they pack the entire Cabela's catalog gear selection with them on stand. Come on, you'll only be there a few hours! The less you bring, the less will get in the way or fall noisily to the ground. Everything you need should fit into an average-sized daypack.

Be Flexible

If you keep seeing game from your stand, but it's out of range, be prepared to move the stand to the area where the game is moving. By mid-morning, if there's no action where you are or if the area's been dead for days, climb down and scout for hot sign. When you find it, move your stand and hunt it that afternoon or the next morning.

Deer do look up! If you move, they'll see you and bolt.

Ground Odor

Game, especially whitetails, will smell where you've walked and will avoid your stand site unless you take great pains to minimize the odor you leave on the ground. Wearing knee-high rubber boots is an important first step. Avoid walking on trails that you think the deer will use to approach your stand. Do not touch anything with your bare skin and wash hunting clothes in no-scent detergent, store them in a clean plastic bag and put them on in the field.

The More, The Merrier

Like many experienced treestand hunters, I believe that the first time you hunt from a stand is your best chance to shoot an animal from it, especially if your goal is a mature buck. So I try to place several different stands each year, hunting specific sites only under perfect conditions. I also love to scout on-the-go with a portable climber or lightweight fixed-position stand, setting it up when I find hot sign and hunting from it that afternoon or the following morning.

Scout from Above

In unfamiliar terrain, I like to take a day and place a treestand in an area where I can overlook a lot of country. My main purpose is to try to observe game movements in the surrounding countryside. If I see a mature animal off in the distance that I want to hunt, I don't hesitate; if the wind's right, I move a stand over to where I saw him and I start hunting.

Use Your Noggin

The big advantage that hunters have over the game we pursue is our ability to outthink them. When selecting a specific tree to place your stand in, put on your thinking cap and ask yourself, "Why this tree?" Have a plan. Anticipate where the game will be traveling and at what angle the stand should be set to your best advantage. Walk a 360-degree circle around the tree before erecting the stand. Decide beforehand how you'll enter and exit the stand location, which branches and limbs to trim and which way the prevailing wind is blowing. Set the stand on the downwind side of the trails that you think the game will use.

The Waiting Game

In truth, I have a love/hate relationship with treestand hunting. I love the chess game: scouting, trying to figure out what the animals are doing and why, the move and countermove of finding a prime location, placing a stand and anticipating what might walk by.

On the other hand, I find that sitting in treestands can be as boring as a slow day in church. I was raised a spot-and-stalk hunter, and unless I can go get 'em, I get a bad case of the fidgets. More than once, after several days of sitting in a stand that I knew was in a great spot and not seeing what I'd hoped to see, I've questioned my sanity and sworn off treestands forever.

And then here he'd come. The king of the woods—white-tailed buck, bull elk, big boar bear or massive mulie—in all his splendor. In those first few seconds when I see him, my heart tries to beat its way out of my chest, my palms drip sweat, my knees knock and my entire body quivers. My composure is shot. Guaranteed!

Whether I get a shot at him—and many times while up in the treestand I've seen the animal that I have dreamed about and have not been able to release an arrow—is immaterial to me. I've won. All the time, effort and sweat equity that went into selecting this particular tree has been worth it. If I'm fortunate enough to shoot ... well, to me, that's gravy.

I know that using a treestand is the best way for me to get into this position. That's why I continue to hunt from them. It's the same reason you should strive to become a safe and skilled treestand hunter, too. ❖

❖ Reality Whitetails ❖

By Tom Carpenter

Even as I near a half century's worth of deer seasons, sleep comes grudgingly—if at all—before opening day.

But now, resting quietly in my sleeping bag, a string of whitetail dream hunts parades through my thoughts. Picking an approved rack from a ranch full of big South Texas bucks, trusty A-Bolt in hand. Tracking a Saskatchewan bruiser through fresh snow and taking him at twilight with my muzzleloader. Waiting alongside a frigid Iowa fenceline for the big 10-pointer that trotted past and then fell to the "whump" of my slug gun. Spending a golden autumn patterning deer during morning and evening treestand bowhunts in the imaginary wooded ridges behind my home, waiting for the buck that I want.

Beep-beep. Beep-beep. Beep-beep. The portable alarm clock ends my slumber.

Dream over. Opening day! I shuffled over to the shack's woodstove, tossed in a couple chunks of popple

and rubbed my eyes. Nice dreams. But not reality. This was reality: an old shack in the woods. Three good friends. Sixty-five acres and some strategically placed stands. Some deer around; maybe a buck, too.

Pulling on long johns, I thought: In exactly two weeks I'd be rising for another state's opener and looking at a parallel reality: two friends' farms, eight miles apart, one 260 acres and the other 200. Good deer country, but not premier. Some company in the field.

If your realities are like my dreams, you're lucky. But who has the dollars, land access and/or time to experience hunts like those? We read about them, but is that your whitetail hunting reality? It's not mine.

Maybe you're saving for a special hunt. Me, too. But until then, and after, there's a lot of whitetail hunting reality to deal with. Limited land—a farm or two, a lease or hunt club with friends, a chunk of land that you own, maybe public land. Limited time—we all need to work for a living and keep a family happy, too, so we have to count our beloved days in the woods carefully. Limited deer—habitat that is probably good but not necessarily crawling with deer to pass up as you wait for something "better."

So what can you do to increase your odds of success, given that you don't have all the money, land or time in the world to hunt?

Here's my reality whitetail hunting checklist. It focuses on firearms hunting, but applies to bowhunting, too. These are just common sense and effective strategies, techniques and tips—ideas that can make success happen for the average-guy hunter. You and me.

Be There

In the end, a successful hunt requires one simple strategy: that you are in the field where you can shoot a deer. Even if it seems like the deer are gone from the acres that you hunt. Even if the weather is bad. Casual hunters overlook this fact; they are the guys who go home without venison.

I have yet to shoot a deer from my couch, or the diner in town, or the warm seat of a pickup truck. If you want to be low-key and leave the woods, fine. But if you're serious about getting a deer, be out there where things can happen.

Dress right and be ready for an all-day stay. Carry a daypack with enough food and water for the day, and extra clothes and disposable body and hand warmers.

Attitude

Whitetails are incredible hiders, which means that there likely are deer very close to you at any given time.

Fifteen to 20 deer live year-round on one of the farms that I mentioned; my farmer friend sees them in the fields on summer evenings. With maybe 80 acres of hiding cover on the place, there's a deer for every four acres, or, theoretically, one within 140 yards of me at all times.

That's what I tell myself when the action is slow and I'm wondering if I'm crazy to be hunting so hard. Do some similar math for your hunting spots. You'll stay out longer and hunt harder.

Instant Success

This relates to attitude: You can be having a miserable hunt one moment, and five seconds later it can be one of your greatest. Think back to some of the deer that

you've shot. Action unfolds quickly. Always be ready for something good to happen. And if bad things happen, don't give up.

A couple years ago, I sat through a blustery and uneventful morning until about 10 a.m., when a group of does loped across a hayfield toward my stand. I leaned against a hickory tree and tried to squeeze off a shot at the lead deer as she paused to test the wind. "Click." I shucked in another shell. "Click." Bad firing pin. Seven white tails flagged goodbye as I cursed my slug gun.

I walked a half-mile back to the truck, retired the slug gun, screwed a rifled choke tube into my little grouse gun and returned to my stand, determined to hunt out the day. During the late afternoon, the wind died down, and a twig cracked behind me.

I hadn't lost hope, and the shotgun was at my shoulder when a spike buck stepped out 20 yards away. "Boom!" And to be honest, there was another "boom" because I missed as he stood but rolled him on his second bound, when it was more like shooting at a grouse. In eight seconds, the day went from bad to great. I was there to make it happen.

Hunt Hard, Hunt Right

That's my pep talk. If you're a reality whitetail hunter, your effort and dedication—being out there, thinking positively and hunting hard and with your heart in it—will be the primary reasons why you either get a deer or go home empty-handed.

Now let's talk a few details. Stick to the simple here, too. Gadgets, gizmos and fancy tricks have yet to bring a reality whitetail to me, anyway.

Know & Love Your Gun

Sight-in your firearm. A magnificent whitetail (they're all magnificent) deserves this respect and a clean kill. You deserve to miss if you don't shoot before the season. But knowing your rifle, shotgun, muzzleloader or bow will also help your attitude and confidence in the woods. One shot, one fleeting chance, is the only link between you and the deer that you've been dreaming about. Make it count.

Late summer is the perfect time to conduct this necessary part of the hunt. Sight-in before other fall hunting seasons occupy your time. Relax. Have fun with it. There's no pressure now. And don't get wigged out about

Mini-drives can be used to move deer when the action is slow. But the idea is to move deer around, not out of, your area. Go quietly. Go slowly.

ballistics and splitting hairs (see "Reality Sighting-In" on next page).

Throw a bullet or slug through the barrel again before the season to be sure that you're still "on."

Scout Right

I won't tell you that scouting is unimportant. But don't traipse around and spook deer away from your hunting area, especially as the season draws near. Set up your stands months before the hunt. If you're hunting a limited amount of land, chances are good that you won't be adjusting their position that much anyway.

Within a month of hunting season, do your spotting and scouting from a distance—from roadways or with binoculars. If possible, use the landowners' knowledge and sightings to tell you where the deer have been living and moving; this traditionally has been my best "scouting" of all.

Hunt Smart

Gear up for comfort so that you can spend the entire day in the woods. Carry a daypack with all the essentials.

You know your hunting land better than I do—where the deer hang out, how to best hunt the terrain. But this approach applies to all reality whitetail hunters: Always take a low-impact approach to your hunting. Be smart about hunting what land you have.

Select your stands carefully and have alternate places to sit for varying winds. Yes, you might have to "overhunt"

a stand; not overhunting stands is a luxury for those who have huge tracts of land to hunt.

Should you do deer drives? That's your call. I will do them—mini-pushes describes the tactic better—when the neighbors are in town having lunch or watching a football game on TV.

The idea is to move deer around, not out of, your hunting area. One hunter pushes. Go quietly. Go slowly. Sneak. My dad was a pro at this. It would take him at least an hour to go 100 yards on a mini-push. But the deer that he moved never hightailed it—they just skulked around him in the woodlot and often enough he'd hear a "boom" from my direction and smile.

He's 83 now, so I push for him, striving to move as slowly and patiently as he did. Bottom line? This plan keeps deer where you can hunt them and not over on the neighbors' property.

We love it when the other hunters in Cadiz Township do their big drives. The little acreage that we hunt benefits from an influx of deer as they escape and then filter back out to their home ranges later. Another reason to stay put and hunt hard all day.

Moments of Truth

Do you know what saves many deer, as many as any other hunter boo-boo? I do. It's ruining the opportunity for a shot before you can even pull the trigger. Jerking the gun up too soon. Or too quickly. Or too late. Or moving too much in the process.

An approaching deer is always a surprise. Try to control your emotions. You might only get this chance. Move slowly but deliberately to get your gun up. Move only when the deer is moving, or when its head is hidden. You'll never win a quick draw. Don't panic or you will surely lose the deer. Be patient, but shoot when the shot is good.

I still get excited while hunting, but this helps: Think "S-S-S-S"—slow-steady-spot-squeeze. *Slow* movements. *Steady* your aim. Aim at one small *spot* on the deer's chest; you know where. *Squeeze* the trigger, don't jerk it. These steps can turn critical moments of truth into moments of success and elation.

Simplify, Enjoy

If you get the idea that I'm not a new-age whitetail hunter, you're right. Other than dressing smartly (good gloves, hat and boots) for the weather conditions at hand, carrying a rifle (or shotgun or muzzleloader) that you trust and a good, sharp knife, what do you really need for successful whitetail hunting? Dedication and a few simple but sound strategies.

And don't let somebody else's standards—on inches of antler or whether there's antler at all—destroy your appreciation of any deer that you are good and lucky enough to take. Remember, this is reality whitetail hunting for real people. What matters is what you think, the record book in your memory.

A Reality Whitetail

Back to opening day. I left the shack early, reached my stand 45 minutes before first light, put on the extra clothes from my day pack and climbed up. Minnesota's November chill crept into my bones, but excitement kept me warm.

A few shots rang out here and there at first light. I waited. It seemed like an eternity. But the woods stayed quiet. I had scouted last spring and had not touched this spot since, except to pass by on a grouse hunt. The light south breeze was just right. It felt good to hold my old rifle.

Reality whitetail hunting success is not measured in inches of antler, but rather memories of quality time spent hunting.

Hoofbeats in the leaves! As I turned slowly, he was there, hidden behind some saplings. My rifle was halfway to my shoulder. Slowly, I raised it up all the way. I could see his white throat patch and eye rings through the scope; I knew where his chest was.

Twenty years ago, I would have shot. But now I waited, so long that my arms began to shake. And then he trotted on past, 30 yards out. Buckskin flashed between tree trunks. I held off. At the last possible moment he paused and then lay quietly on his side, and I realized that I'd shot.

I waited a few minutes, wondering if I was still dreaming. But I wasn't. This was real. I climbed down and walked over to the buck, smiling. The sun's first rays cleared the popple and oak trees as I knelt beside him and held his thick little 8-point antlers, thinking—this buck makes me happier than any dream. ❖

Reality Sighting-In

You can study ballistics tables for hours, fret over fractions of inches and shoot until your shoulder is raw. Or you can follow these simple sighting-in guidelines and take the pressure off.

12 Gauge Slug Gun: With a rifled barrel and saboted slugs, sight-in 2 inches high at 50 yards; you can hold right on to 100 yards. With a choke tube or smooth barrel and regular rifled slugs, use the same sight-in but hold right on, out to only 75 yards.

Rifle: For woods and brush hunting, sight-in to be dead on at 50 or 100 yards. Either way, you'll be right on for any shot that you encounter. There's nothing like knowing exactly where that bullet is going in these situations. When longer shots are possible, sight-in to be 2 inches high (no more) at 100 yards. I don't care what caliber you're shooting, you'll be dead on at 200 to 230 yards with everything from a .270 Win. on up; that's plenty far.

Muzzleloader: Use the shotgun guideline: 2 inches high at 50 yards. You'll be good out to 100, maybe beyond, but check first.

❖ SECOND-CHANCE BUCKS ❖

By John L. Sloan

It was mid-January, and the rut was in full swing. Bucks were chasing does everywhere, even to the point of exhaustion. That morning, from a stand tucked into an old fenceline, I saw nine deer—seven does and two bucks. Both bucks were hot on the trail of does. That afternoon, from a stand overlooking a green field nestled between a grown-up clear-cut and a broad band of hardwoods, I watched as four good bucks chased 10 does, and each other, around.

Reports such as this are not unusual in mid-November. For most of the country, this is when the whitetail rut peaks and the highest percentage of does are bred. Once the rut is over, some hunters give up on their chances to kill a trophy buck. Some even stop hunting. There are a few, however, who make plans to head south.

This was the case with three guys from New Jersey. Having filled their tags back home, they came to Red Oak Plantation for a second chance at a trophy. Between them, they killed four does and two nice bucks.

Red Oak, the sister operation of the famed White Oak Plantation, located just outside Tuskegee, Alabama, is in the heart of an area of the country with a late rut. It is not a second rut or a phase of a long-running rut period. In this part of the country, and in others, the rut doesn't begin until after Christmas. And that, coupled with easy access and moderate rates, gives hunters a second chance to hunt the peak of the rut.

Most hunters are aware that the Texas rut peaks in January. But stories of high prices and large trophy fees deter many from hunting there. No doubt about it, there are huge bucks in Texas, but hunting them can be expensive. I was recently on a hunt at a large ranch that charged a $3,500 trophy fee for bucks 11 points or larger. Much of the South, where some of the finest hunting lodges are located, has a later rut, too. In portions of Alabama, Mississippi, Georgia and Louisiana, the rut peaks in January. And the cost for a hunt at most of these lodges is modest.

Alabama operations such as White Oak, Red Oak,

Sedgefield and others cater to this late-season crowd. They offer a choice of hunting with a gun or bow, but understand that the tactics for each are different. Other lodges, such as Tara Plantation and Willow Point in Mississippi and Louisiana, offer bowhunting only. There are some public hunting grounds in the South, but they see quite a bit of pressure.

Most of the lodges are under trophy management programs, ensuring a chance at a good buck. To find public land, your best bet is to contact the wildlife agencies in the states where you are interested in hunting. To find the right lodge, read advertisements in magazines like *North American Hunter*, and then check references. You can expect to pay $1,000 to $2,000 for a five-day hunt.

There are two advantages to hunting the Deep South rut. Northern hunters get a second chance at a big, rutting buck. And it is a welcome break from ice, snow and frigid weather. But don't be fooled. Thirty-degree temperatures in Alabama can freeze you to death. Take warm clothes.

An ice storm was paralyzing the Midwest. Buffalo had 10 inches of snow. Boston was just about shut down, and I was sweating as I watched a big doe enter a green field 235 yards away. I was in shirtsleeves. Because of the 80-degree heat, I was not expecting bucks to start chasing does in daylight, so I shot her. Twenty minutes later, my .270 Win. put another doe on the ground. It was January 11, and cold weather was forecast for the next day. That afternoon, a hunter reported seeing two bucks chase a doe until they all had to bed down and rest, including the hunter.

Most Southern deer operations have a common problem: Hunters won't kill enough does to ensure a good buck/doe ratio. So liberal bag limits allow for plenty of opportunities to fill your freezer. But on the cold, frosty mornings and in the late, cooling afternoons, watch for bucks.

No matter where you are or when it is, the tactics for hunting the rut are the same. First, you need to find a

Southern rut hunting is no different than in the North. Always be on your toes, because you never know when that trophy buck is going to cross your path.

Bowhunting the Late Rut

Bowhunting a late, Southern rut is, at least on the surface, the same as gun hunting. The only difference is that you must get closer. For that reason, I like to take my own stands when bowhunting at these lodges. As a bowhunter, I can't reach out across a field, so I am forced to ambush deer as they come to it. Sometimes, that requires hanging a new stand. I always check with the lodge managers to make sure that they will permit me to use my own stand. If the lodge offers both gun and bowhunting, then bucks will have had a month or more of hunting pressure by the time that the rut hits. I like to move a stand back into the timber as much as 100 yards for bowhunting in the afternoon. Moving or hanging a new stand can do wonders for your odds of ambushing and killing a buck.

But an ambush is not the only way to hunt these bucks. Just as it is anywhere else, now is the time for scents, calling and rattling. Now is when you can move a buck 100 yards or more with a doe bleat or some light rattling. This is the time to drag a scent rag and place a scent bomb near your stand. In Pennsylvania, Iowa, Illinois or Minnesota, as well as other states, the rut is the rut. The tactics are the same. It just occurs two months later in the South.

As a general rule, when I rattle in the South, I use a rattle bag or a set of light antlers. Although there are some bruiser bucks in every Southern state, there aren't as many as you might find in the Midwest or Canada, so I tone things down. As for calling, I almost exclusively use doe bleats during the rut. The only time I will challenge a buck with a grunt call is when I can see him and can tell that he is not going to come any closer to the bleat. As for scents, I use any good doe-in-heat product, and I use it primarily on a drag rag. I then hang the rag near my stand.

The South is not composed only of green fields. Most operations also have corn or bean fields. One of the biggest deer magnets I have ever seen was a huge, picked cotton field. One frigid morning, I could hear a nice 8-point buck chasing a doe across the frozen, rock hard ground 30 seconds before I could see him. Unfortunately, the cotton field was on another piece of

food source. Then isolate the travel patterns to it. In the mornings, hunt the woods. In the afternoons, hunt the fields; providing that there are fields. In the South, hunting near food plots is the most effective way to ambush a rutting buck. Does will come to the green fields and bucks will come to the does. This is where "bean-field" rifles come in handy. Shots longer than 250 yards are not uncommon. Good optics are a must when judging the quality of a buck in low light conditions. But what if you are bowhunting?

property. But agricultural crops, as well as green fields, are prime, big-time magnets once the mast has been depleted. These are the afternoon stand sites. They're not the best places to rattle, but in the afternoons I prefer to sit quietly and wait.

That, you see, is a Southern tradition—sitting quietly and waiting. It is a slower paced lifestyle, filled with good food, laughter and plenty of Southern hospitality. And, of course, it also gives hunters a second chance at hunting the peak of the rut.

Pick up the phone today. Wouldn't you like to have a second chance? ❖

SOUTHERN WHITETAILS CAN BE DIFFICULT TO HUNT
By David Morris

Deer hunting traditions run deep in the South. High deer densities, long seasons, liberal bag limits and a large rural population make deer hunting an important part of Southern culture. The South is a diverse region; habitats vary from rugged mountains and vast river swamps, to gently rolling hills of broken forests and flat, monoculture piney woods. Most hunting is done on private land, and trophy management on varying levels is increasing throughout the region.

As a result of the lack of age and good nutrition, the average size antlers of mature bucks in the South is about 110 Boone and Crockett Club points. Trophy status starts at 120, and anything more than 130 is exceptional. Though bigger ones are taken there, 140 is pretty much the realistic top-end.

As for huntability, the South is slightly harder than average to hunt. Thick, leafy cover adds an element of difficulty. Heavy pressure, worsened in areas by hunters using dogs to hunt and long seasons, causes deer to move at first and last light, or at night. Even the typically warm weather encourages only nocturnal movement. Without food plots or agriculture crops to expose and concentrate deer, the South can prove to be a frustrating place to hunt.

❖ Hunting the Mule Deer Rut ❖

By Bob Robb

Whitetail hunters believe that the rut is a magical time, when they have their best chance of the entire season to take a mature buck. Generally, this thinking is right on the money. When the breeding urge takes over, caution is often thrown to the wind, because even the most secretive buck has no choice but to answer nature's call.

While you can find a library full of information dealing with rut hunting tactics for whitetails, there's little available on the importance of hunting the rut for mule deer and its coastal cousin, the Columbia blacktail. Is that because hunting during the breeding season is a less effective way to locate, and harvest, mature bucks of these two deer species?

Not on your life. Just as it is when hunting big whitetails, the mule deer rut can be your best chance of the year to take the buck of your dreams.

Mule Deer Rut Behavior

The rutting season occurs during late fall. Depending on the latitude, this can be anywhere from early November to late December and January. When planning a rut hunt for mulies and blacktails in new country, it pays to call area biologists to determine when the rut generally occurs and when its peak is anticipated.

Like a whitetail, a mule deer buck will during courtship test a doe's readiness for breeding by obtaining a urine sample. According to noted wildlife biologist and author Dr. Valerius Geist, mule deer are the only ungulates that have two methods of obtaining this urine sample. The first is the familiar "low stretch" approach, where the buck approaches the female from behind in a low stretched posture, licking his nose and uttering soft calls, similar to a fawn distress call. He might then touch the female with his muzzle. The female acts as if she's ignoring him, feeding and moving in small half circles. The courtship continues until the female urinates, at which time the buck moves in and "lip-curls" to determine the doe's readiness for breeding.

The second method occurs when the buck becomes impatient as he waits for the doe to urinate. He might throw what Geist describes as a "temper tantrum." His body becomes stiff, his upper lip begins to quiver, and a high-pitched tone resonates from deep within his throat. The buck might then throw himself, antlers lowered, at the courted female, all the while roaring. When she takes off, he follows on her heels, slams the ground with his front legs and bellows with every jump. After a couple hundred yards, this chase usually ends with the buck resuming the low stretch position, and the female usually urinating.

During the rut, mule deer herds exhibit a characteristic more commonly associated with elk. The does, badgered by every testosterone-overloaded juvenile buck in the region, often stay close to the dominant buck and seek his protection from unwanted advances. The smaller bucks often circle the herd, just like young "satellite" bull elk, waiting for their chance to sneak in and satisfy their breeding urge. The difference between elk and mule deer is that the dominant buck doesn't control the does like a bull elk controls a harem of cows. Instead, he's interested in one specific doe at a time, which is the one in, or closest to, estrus.

When a buck and a doe breed, they usually isolate themselves from the larger group of does for a day or two. The doe's estrous period lasts about a day, during which time she's repeatedly bred. Naturally, smaller bucks crisscrossing the range looking for does might come upon the pair, in which case they try to split them up so that they can do some breeding, too.

The bulk of the mule deer rut lasts three to four weeks. During this time the older breeding bucks lose a lot of their physical strength, often breaking antler points and receiving tears in their coats from fighting, and appearing listless and dazed near the end of the cycle. When they quit breeding—they often quit cold turkey in one day—they become isolated, looking for thick bedding cover in which they can recuperate

Like whitetails, mule deer fights can be fierce when a hot doe is at stake.

enough strength to survive the winter. Post-rut behavior sees bucks disperse, rest for about three or four weeks, then emerge when it's time to shed their antlers and battle winter. They often join doe herds at this time, seeking the security from predators that large numbers of animals bring.

Basic Rut Hunt Tactics

During the rut, mature mule deer bucks lose much of the caution that dominates their lives during the rest of the year. Bucks that wouldn't think of being caught out in the open and away from the dark timber or thick brush where they live during daylight hours, now are seen moving across open sage flats and bare hillsides searching for does in estrus.

The hunter can use this behavior to his advantage in several ways. In open and semi-open terrain, the best technique is to climb to a high vantage point and carefully glass the surrounding countryside for deer. This is true for both mule deer and blacktails. Once a herd of does—at this time of year they're like buck magnets—is located, take your time and glass both the herd and the surrounding hills for a buck. If you don't spot one right

away, don't despair. He might be isolated and breeding a doe in a nearby coulee or thicket. I remember one Utah muzzleloader hunt during November in which my partner and I checked on a herd of two dozen does every day for a week until finally, the day before we were to head home, a dandy buck appeared in their midst. Good things, as they say, often come to those who wait. If you spot only fair-to-middlin' bucks with the does, don't give up.

It should be noted that most rut behavior occurs on or near the winter range. This lower-elevation terrain can be everything from sage brush flats to cedar and juniper jungles, to open hillsides or croplands. Learning where this winter range is—and, therefore, where the deer are likely to be—prior to hunting is important to your success.

If the deer are on private land, obtaining permission to hunt is vital. If permission isn't possible, you can often hunt those deer off the private ground and on public land, where the deer sometimes go to bed in brushy draws and hillsides. I shot a big buck with my bow one year in New Mexico out of a large herd that followed a set routine every day. The deer fed in an alfalfa field at dawn and lingered there for a couple of hours before departing the private ground and moving to adjacent juniper-and brush-covered public land hills to bed for the day. I laid ambush after ambush for that buck, only to be busted by one of his 40-some companions for seven straight days. A light snow dusted the ground on the eighth day, when I found them bedded in the junipers. I slowly sneaked within 45 yards of the bedded deer and grunted the buck to his feet and 20 yards closer before my arrow found its mark.

That brings us to the next phase of rut hunting—calling.

Calling Mulies & Blacktails

Calling whitetails by using vocal sounds or rattling has been an accepted hunting technique for many years. Yet many hunters are still amazed that you can do the same thing with mulies and blacktails.

And why not? All deer species are vocal; emitting grunts, squeaks and squeals at varying times. Mulies and blacktails will lock antlers and battle like it was Super

Gregg Gutschow found this Powder River, Montana, buck loafing with a hot doe during the mid-November rut.

Bowl Sunday during the rut. They'll rake their antlers on small conifers, cedars and junipers and engage in mock battle with brush. And just like calling whitetails, hunters must pick the time and place to use calling techniques. The rut is that time.

One of the best techniques for taking those big, supersleuth black-tailed bucks that live in the Pacific Northwest's rainforest jungles is to rattle them in during the rut. Many of these hunts are restricted to archery and blackpowder, but in the heavy cover where these deer live in and in which you must hunt, shots are generally short.

I've found that both rattling and calling work best in relatively thick cover, which can be anything from thick timber stands to deep brushy canyons and draws to coastal rainforest fauna. In open country, like sagebrush flatlands, I've had little success with rattling and virtually none with calling, unless it's to a buck that I already spotted and stalked near. With mule deer, my preferred method is to spot them before they see me and stalk in for a shot. But calling and rattling worked for me when I was not able to locate deer living in the thick stuff. It's worth considering—even though both are "whitetail" tactics.

The mule deer rut is a magical time, especially for mule deer hunters. It's not a time for freezer hunting, though, of course, the delicious meat is a welcome addition to the larder. Instead, it's a time to observe the deer and learn about them. It's also a time to hold out for the buck of your life. There's no better time to find him! ❖

"DISPUTED" CHAMPION
OF THE DEER WORLD

By Jim Shockey

Discussions about which deer species is the most difficult to hunt invariably end nowhere; mostly because the majority of us are either whitetail hunters or mule deer hunters and are incapable (myself excluded) of being objective (as a journalist, I am required to report objectively).

The truth of the matter is, while both whitetails and mule deer have their good and bad points (although everyone knows that mule deer have more bad points), neither is the toughest to hunt. In fact (in my opinion), mule deer and whitetails are the easiest of the deer species to hunt, even easier than Sitka deer and way easier than Coues' deer.

That leaves only one species, the "disputed" champion of the deer world. The Columbia black-tailed deer is (in my opinion) the most difficult deer species to hunt. Hunting one of these wraiths is a lesson in humility, one that I have learned all too well, thank you very much. It took this whitetail hunter 10 seasons, hunting in prime blacktail country in the mountains of the West Coast, to see the light and admit the awful truth. I was unworthy! Unless I got some professional help or found a messed up black-tailed buck (one with a mule deer brain), I'd never hang my tag on a big Columbia blacktail.

Oregon or Bust

Fortunately for all us "outclassed" whitetail and mule deer hunters, there are outfitters (masochists) who specialize in guiding for Columbia blacktails. One of the best is Doug Gattis, owner of Southern Oregon Game Busters. Once I accepted that I had a problem and needed help, the road to recovering my self-esteem was obvious. It started with a call to Doug to book a hunt. Unfortunately, the first time, I made the mistake of scheduling the blacktail hunt with Doug right after my Saskatchewan whitetail season and ran into technical difficulties and couldn't make it. (Orders from my wife.

She seemed to think that four straight months of hunting was enough.)

Needless to say, that year Doug's hunters killed several monster blacktails in the 140 Boone and Crockett Club class, including a monster taken by *North American Hunter* columnist Bob Robb. Unfortunately, while Bob was tagging his gagger Columbia blacktail, I was at home paying bills, driving the kids to school and being a good husband and missed the action. Needless to say, I had high hopes of similar success when I booked the hunt for the next year. Or I did until I stepped off the airplane in Medford, Oregon, and had my hopes broiled away by a blazing sun that was doing its best to turn the Coastal rainforests of Oregon into the Sahara Desert.

It was pretty evident that even with Doug's professional help, my odds of killing a camel were better than my odds of tagging a trophy blacktail. In spite of the fact that we still-hunted our way up and down some of the most beautiful country to be found at the epicenter of the global warming trend, I didn't touch the trigger of my Knight muzzleloader. Doug showed me dozens of deer, none of which were willing to become blacktail burgers. And none that were as large as the 9 or 10 huge black-tailed bucks that we saw every day hanging around Doug's house! I even remember some of their names: Bucky, Eyeguard, Big Boy and the Psycho twins. They walked around in the middle of the day, posing for my video camera, safe as babies, because ... why? It suddenly occurred to me to ask the obvious question.

"Doug?" I asked nicely, as I peered through my viewfinder.

"Yes?" Doug answered.

"Is it legal to hunt right here in your backyard?"

"Yep. Go ahead if you want," he said. "Never could shoot a buck with a name, myself."

In spite of knowing that the bucks were taking unfair advantage of the hunting ethic, neither could I.

A Second Opinion

Busted by the unseasonably warm weather in Oregon and humbled once again by the black-tailed deer's ability to do whatever it takes to survive the hunting season, including hiding out in a blacktail outfitter's backyard, I was still badly in need of professional help. Naturally, I sought out the man behind the name that continually crops up in Columbia blacktail hunting circles—Jim Schaafsma, owner of Arrow Five Outfitters.

Jim and his wife, Tina Marie, live in Columbia

The author swallowed his pride, sought help and took this California buck with Arrow Five Outfitters.

BORDERLINE BLACKTAILS

By Gregg Gutschow

Less than 100 miles from the southernmost Columbia black-tailed deer border recognized by the Boone and Crockett Club are a bunch of deer that deserve better than to be categorized as mule deer. They look like blacktails. Worse yet, they act like blacktails.

Last fall, I got to see them for myself as a guest of Weatherby Firearms on a sprawling, hill-country ranch near Parkfield, California. Toting a .30-06 and expect-

Gregg Gutschow, left, and Weatherby's Brad Ruddell survey the California hills for deer.

ing some mixed-up blacktail/mule deer hybrids, I figured the August deer hunting to be easy.

I'd been blacktail hunting before, in northern California with Arrow Five Outfitters. That time, I was in B&C's designated blacktail zone and carried a bow. Youch. I never got within reasonable bow range of a mature buck despite the fact that I saw good bucks every day of the hunt. We'd spot them, play the wind, stalk them, get to the ambush, and they'd be gone. God knows where.

So, suffice to say I had a healthy chip on my shoulder heading into my hunt with Weatherby's Brad Ruddell farther south. The Outfitter Custom rifle topped with a Weaver Grand Slam scope felt reassuring slung over my shoulder. These hybrid blacktails, I figured, were in grave danger.

A couple days into the hunt, I realized that B&C's border doesn't mean much to the deer. They had the same sickening stealth that their northern counterparts had. Nocturnal tendencies; impenetrable bedding areas; and a safety-in-numbers personality that made it impossible to pin down a lone, big buck.

It was 90-some degrees during the days, and I was

black-tailed deer heaven near Zenia, a small town in northern coastal California. Their hunters take some awesome blacktails, true blacktails recognized by B&C. I'd hunted Coues' deer with the Schaafsmas in Old Mexico and believed that I knew them well enough to request a little help.

"Please! You gotta help me! Please!" I wouldn't call it begging exactly, more like asking in a pleading manner ... from a groveling position on my knees.

Before you can say "load up the truck and head to Beverly," I was on my way to the Schaafsma ranch to hunt huge Columbia blacktails.

"There's one," Tina Marie said, peering through her binoculars. "Under that live oak across the valley."

"Sure is," Jim agreed.

"Right. I see it." I didn't see it.

"There's another buck just under the ridge," Jim said.

"Uh huh. See it, too," Tina Marie confirmed.

"Yep. Got it." I hadn't got it.

"Big one! Lying in the shade down the trail, near the creek!" Jim said.

"Nice one all right," Tina Marie confirmed.

"Down the trail." I poured over the landscape, searching for something, anything that looked like a deer and didn't see a thing.

"Near the creek. Right. I see it." Not.

That first day on the Schaafsma ranch in November taught me a valuable lesson about Columbia black-tailed deer hunting—the little son-of-a-guns are hard to see! Tina Marie and Jim spotted them by the dozen, literally, while I got blisters on my eyeballs trying to

hot under the collar. If not for the wonderful diversions of first-rate wild hog hunting and hundreds of eager ground squirrels, I'd have waved a white flag at the deer and floored it for the airport.

But one evening I got two lucky breaks. A sharp-tusked, long-tailed, black wild boar pushing 250 pounds appeared in the golden wild oats and star this-tle, plowing a path toward water. Brad knew the hole where the pig was going, and we angled to a hilltop vantage that would put us within 100 yards. The first shot was a slam-dunk perfectly through the lungs, but it took two more with the pig at full throttle to stop the muscle machine. Pictures and field dressing took until the final hour of daylight.

With the great hog on the front rack of the Jeep, we cornered a ranch road, and I grabbed guide Robert Palm's shoulder as he hammered the brakes. Up ahead, under an oak, stood a nice 3-point blacktail, err, mule deer ... whatever. I rubbed my eyes—a standing-still blacktail in the open! We bailed out, circled and eased closer.

The shot anchored the buck, and it all seemed too easy right then. But then came a flood of memories of

The author with a 3-point buck technically classified as a mule deer, but with all the bad habits of a blacktail.

dozens of blacktail stalks gone bad, and I admired this southern California buck with as much respect as I've ever held for any big game animal.

Some day, when I'm in a really masochistic kind of mood, I'm going to go back to Columbia blacktail country armed with my bow. Even if I come home with another unfilled blacktail tag, I'm going to return a better bowhunter. Blacktails have a way of bringing out the best in you.

find even one. By the end of the day, they'd spotted 30 different bucks, and I'd spotted one. On day two, I started to get the knack of picking the deer out of the shadows, and by day three I was all over the little rascals. The Schaafsmas only out-spotted me by a factor of 10-to-1.

Each day we'd head into the hills and glass for rutting bucks. When we would (Jim and Tina Marie would) spot a big-enough buck, we'd make a stalk. We (they) saw an average of 35 bucks per day with a high of 50 different bucks one day! But unfortunately, things didn't go my way. One large buck that Jim had been seeing every day prior to my arrival disappeared the day I got there. Another huge buck was swallowed up by a freak fog bank one morning, and at least three others disappeared seconds before I was about to pull the trigger.

I'd spend the middle of the day still-hunting and then would hit the binoculars with the Schaafsmas again during the late afternoon. It finally happened on the last day. A monster of a 4x4 stood up from its bed as I still-hunted through the oak forest. Although neither Jim nor Tina Marie were there to help me judge it, there was no doubt that it was a world record, far bigger than any blacktail that I'd ever actually sneaked up on in 10 years of hunting them. In one motion, I lifted my Knight muzzleloader and fired. BOOM! The buck dropped in its tracks, but as I walked up to it, right before my very eyes, I witnessed it "shape change" into a somewhat smaller buck!

The good news was, I was thrilled. The buck was still larger than any other Columbia blacktail that I'd taken. The bad news was, since I knew that there were much larger bucks on the ranch, I needed to figure out a way to come back the next year. The other good news was I hadn't forgotten how to "ask in a pleading manner."

"Please! Can I come back? Please?"

A Second Chance

Before you can say "loaded up the truck and moved to Beverly," I was back at Arrow Five, this time with my entire family. The pictures that I'd taken the year before, showing the Schaafsmas' quaint antler-clad lodge tucked in a shaded corner of the ranch,

was enough to convince the crew that they should accompany me for a late-August hunt. After the 20-hour drive, as soon as we opened the doors and said "hi" to the Schaafsmas, my family scattered—my son to look for lizards, my daughter to follow a wild pig family across the yard and my wife to the veranda. I took to the hills to look for a bigger blacktail than the one that I'd taken the year before.

The leaves of live oak hide blacktails, and the acorns provide food.

"There he is," Tina Marie said. We hadn't been gone from the ranch house and my family for more than an hour when Tina Marie spotted the first buck.

"Yep. You bet. I see him." I didn't see him.

"He's shed his velvet since this morning," Jim added after checking out the buck out more closely. "Are you ready to shoot a deer so early in your hunt?"

Ready to shoot? Was Jim serious? After all the years that I'd put in trying to find a really big blacktail, was I ready to shoot? I was ready to crawl across a mile of broken glass during the first second of the hunt if that's what I had to do!

The buck that we'd (they'd) spotted was actually a buck that they'd seen for several days in a row, bedding along a low ridge in the valley bottom. In August, Tina Marie explained, the black-tailed bucks tend to stay put in one spot or very close to it. That morning she had seen the big 5x4 again while scouting for me. It had been in full velvet then, but now, as we worked our way closer, and I could actually see the buck, it was obvious that the buck was "hard-horned." Its antlers shone like polished mahogany in the mid-afternoon sun.

BOOM! For the second year in a row, I aimed at a

big California blacktail and touched the trigger of my muzzleloader, sending the Nosler bullet on its devastating way. Five minutes later, after all the years of trying, I finally held in my hands the toughest of the deer to hunt—a big, mature Columbia black-tailed buck.

Author's note: My son took a great wild hog on the second day of our stay with the Schaafsmas. Then, since the hunt was over and we had several days left in our trip, we headed for civilization in search of something that my wife and daughter assured me also existed in abundance in California ... designer discount stores. ❖

Shockey's second California blacktail scored well up in the Longhunter Society record book and saved him from having to suffer more blacktail hunting humiliation.

TURKEY
ADDICTION

It's an exquisite sort of torture, this turkey hunting.

In the spring you're up hours before the sun, trying to get yourself into position for a gobbler at dawn. Sleep deprivation—because you were likely out at dusk as well, trying to put a tom to bed—becomes a fact of life. Yet there's nowhere else you'd rather be on a fine spring morning than out in the turkey woods with the leaves unfurling and the world coming to life again.

In the fall you're working yourself to the bone—walking and walking or waiting and waiting for those phantom flocks that you just can't seem to catch up with. The miles and the hours add up big-time.

But to hear an answer to your calls. To work a turkey. To see that bright red, white or blue head bobbing through the woods as you slip off the safety and stare down your shotgun barrel as the blood pounds through your head. That's where a turkey addict gets his or her fix.

❖ SETTING UP FOR SUCCESS ❖

By Mark Kayser

Being consistently successful requires a thought-out strategy and a well-executed game plan.

Does "Monday Night Football" draw your attention like the lovesick call of a hen turkey draws the attention of a pack of jakes? Okay, but do you really watch the game? I mean really watch it. Each team comes prepared with a carefully orchestrated strategy designed to defeat its opponent. It's the same with turkey hunting. Okay, not exactly the same. You won't have helmet-clad turkeys rushing your offensive line. But if you don't go onto the playing field with proven strategies for your setup, a seasoned gobbler will find holes in your game plan and his instinctive defenses will give him the edge.

Going into the turkey woods with a detailed strategy isn't as easy as hunting whitetails from a stationary treestand. When chasing whitetails, a hunter has the advantage of scouting an area beforehand. He can select stands that offer clear shooting lanes and good concealment. Turkey hunting is a game that's often measured in split-second decisions. Often, you must quickly decide where to plunk your butt as a gobbler speedily approaches in search of the hen that he heard moments earlier. So how does a hunter win this game of ever-changing playing fields?

Turkeys are almost constantly on the move, and to be successful, hunters need to move with them. When the time finally comes to sit down for the final setup, success often depends on being able to quickly analyze the situation and apply solid tactics. Even a helmet-clad gobbler will have a tough time surviving a load of copper-plated No. 5s from a hunter using strategy-wise setups.

Study the Terrain

Whether you are sneaking through the woods trying to entice a tom to answer a call or staking out a roosted gobbler, pay close attention to the lay of the land. Turkeys, like most wild critters, know every inch of their turf and they utilize routes that offer easy traveling with few obstacles.

Hunters who chase gobblers in hilly country know

If a stubborn gobbler hangs up and refuses to come to the call, the hunter must often make a mad dash to relocate.

the difficulties of getting a bird to climb a steep ridge or descend into a dark, scary hollow. Odds are good that the bird won't budge; instead, he'll gobble like crazy in hopes that the hen will come to him. And in the turkey's world, that's the way it works. A gobbler positions himself so that hens can hear and see him. The instinctively programmed hen then goes to the gobbler.

Steep slopes and deep holes aren't the only barriers that block a gobbler's approach. Rivers also present a barrier to most turkeys. I can't count the number of times that I've had gobblers hang up across a river from me and strain their vocal cords trying to get the "hen" to cross.

One May morning, I coaxed a gobbler to the opposite bank of a river. Hidden in some brush, I used every imaginable call to get him onto the runway for the commuter flight across. I created a ruckus of yelps, fighting purrs, gobbles and wing beats. The excited tom gobbled and paced the riverbank. He even backed up a few times with the looks of making a run for flight. In the end, though, we both ended up with sore throats and a firm commitment to holding our own

terra firma.

Not all bodies of water represent such an ominous barrier. Small creeks, marshy areas and ponds might slow a gobbler down, but if you can cross or circum-navigate a water source, odds are high that a gobbler can do the same.

Another common barrier is the woven-wire fence. You'd think that a critter equipped with wings would just fly over such an inconvenience, but instead, a turkey's peanut-sized brain tells him to pace the fence like a zoo-caged lion. Roads, on the other hand, don't seem to be a problem. Although I once found a hotspot near a busy highway where a turkey fell prey to the Michelin Man about once a week.

Perfect Positioning

After eyeing the terrain and deciding on a general area to sit, a hunter's brain needs to go into overdrive and analyze the site with computer-like speed for a perfect setup. If a gobbler is charging the call, time is of the essence. Even a roosted bird requires setup speed, as each minute of daylight brightens the landscape.

Does the area offer enough concealment to lure a

Moving In

While three or four strands of barbed wire looks open to you, this can be a major obstacle for turkeys. You can slowly crawl closer to the fence and shoot from the prone position. Turkeys have keen eyesight; stay low, move slowly and listen to the gobbling or footsteps to keep informed of the gobbler's location. Stay alert for other hunters if you move in on a gobbler. Here, the hunter realizes that there is a fence between him and the tom. The hunter crawls carefully closer, then tries to lure the tom into shooting range.

Tom is hung up and reluctant to cross the fence, so hunter carefully moves closer to the fence.

Tom struts close to fence at times, but will not cross it.

searching gobbler in close? Does the brush offer enough openings for a clear shot? Is there enough cover to hide a human form and protect it in case another hunter stalks the calls?

As noted above, it's abnormal for most gobblers to frantically run through the woods searching for love. In the real world, they sit back, gobble, show off and get the girl in the end. In the hunter's world, however, we want them to do the searching and traveling. Be sure that the setup you choose offers plenty of cover between you and the gobbler's position. If he can see the calling site and doesn't see a hen, he might hang up out of shotgun range.

My best setups include areas just inside a strip of brush or timber. This terrain makes the gobbler stick his head into the brush to find the hen. The next best tactic is to employ decoys. In fact, in either scenario, I usually stake a decoy out to give the gobbler something to focus on and divert his attention from me in case I need to make a last-second shooting adjustment.

Make sure that the brush isn't too thick for a clear shot. A cagey gobbler might come in close, but too much brush can restrict your shot or block it from hitting the target. One of my hunting buddies who specializes in bowhunting turkeys always carries a folding saw and pruning shears. Since the slightest twig can hamper arrow flight, he'll clip small shooting lanes if time allows. Sometimes all it takes is simply breaking off a few branches to clear the way, but be sure to eye down the barrel and confirm that you have open shooting lanes.

Finally, when deciding where to sit, be sure to consider your safety. Even in sparsely populated South Dakota, where I live, hunters stalk turkey calls and that sets the stage for disaster. Most savvy hunters sit against a tree trunk that is big enough to cover their entire back in case someone sneaks in from behind and takes a pot-shot at an incoming bird or even the decoy.

Several years back, a buddy of mine staked a decoy out and plunked down beside a tree, hoping to lure a flock that followed a regular travel route. The warm, spring sunshine caused him to drop into a hunter's nap, but that nap abruptly ended at the crack of a varmint rifle as a distant hunter spied his decoy. Shooting

Don't hit the turkey woods without creature comforts: an organized vest, a shotgun rest, and a good seat cushion.

turkeys with a rifle is legal in South Dakota. The shooter, quickly realizing his mistake, retreated over the hill while my shaken buddy tried to gather his composure.

Creature Comforts

Even though most setups come about quickly, go afield with your gear organized and be prepared to sit for long periods. Not all birds rush in like those you see on the hunting shows. Some take their sweet time.

I never go afield without a cushion for my backside. My favorite seat has a self-filling air cushion and straps to my turkey vest to ensure that it will never fall by the wayside on a hasty turkey trek. Hunter's Specialties designed the vest and cushion with other options besides comfort. It also offers the advantage of being more organized than a lazy Susan in Martha Stewart's TV kitchen.

A cushion will increase the length of time that a hunter can wait out a bird, but another useful item that I've discovered is a strap-on shotgun rest that attaches to my leg. With the knee bent up in a typical

turkey setup, it allows you to balance your shotgun in the general direction of the turkey without the hassles of it slipping off a rounded kneecap.

Finally, choose a camouflage pattern that blends in with the terrain no matter if you're sitting against a tree or lying in the grass along a meadow. There is no excuse for not finding a pattern that matches your hunting neighborhood; a well-camoed hunter completes a successful setup.

Although I'm not a huge fan of "Monday Night Football," I've watched enough to learn that football can cause grown men to paint their bodies in the colors of their home team. More importantly, I've learned that sound strategies win games. For turkey hunters, a sound setup will lay the groundwork for a winning strategy and success. Even though the competition is equipped with a peanut-sized brain, its survival instinct elevates it to genius status, capable of making a turkey hunter look as foolish as a grown man on national television with his face painted blue and orange. ❖

❖ THE DARK SIDE OF DECOYS ❖

By Scott Bestul

Watching a turkey that's been hoodwinked by a decoy is always fun, but few of these occasions are as memorable as the one I encountered during a Wisconsin hunt two years ago. I was guiding a bowhunter who was after his first tom, and he insisted that we hunt out of a blind resembling a canvas Army wall tent. I'm no cutt-'n'-run turkey caller, but I don't spend a lot of time on

a seat cushion, either; so sitting in that blind the first day had me a little edgy. But on the second morning, I was thinking differently.

We set up before dawn, just uphill from where a gobbler was booming lustily on his roost. We'd managed to sneak within 100 yards of him and found, miraculously, that an old logging road led roughly from his tree to the corner of a small field. The spot screamed "ambush," so we scrambled to set up the tent before flydown.

Once inside the tent, I gave a soft tree yelp to let the tom know that we were in his neighborhood. His chuckling gobble assured us that he was good to go, but the soft yelping of a hen roosted nearby quickly sank our spirits.

"Maybe you can call 'em both in," my hunter whispered.

"Yeah, maybe," I muttered skeptically.

But the hen behaved wonderfully. More eager to join us than the gobbler, she pitched out of the tree and waltzed up the logging road, waddling joyously into the decoys. The gobbler followed, alternately strutting and walking, his husky beard sweeping up morning dew. When he hit 30 yards, I whispered, "Take him," and then remembered that my guy was shooting aluminum, not lead. The hen cooed and clucked lovingly among our setup, pecking first near our two hens, then sidling up to the jake that we'd placed within a few feet of the blind. Staring out the shooting window, I realized that I'd never been so close to a wild, living turkey. For your information, when a turkey blinks, its bottom eyelids reach up to meet the top ones.

The gobbler continued to hang either just out of bow range or managed to keep his vitals obscured by grass. The hen continued to gossip with her foam

Even though it's common to use decoys to attract toms (above), decoys can also be effective tools to entice hens (inset) and toms often follow hens.

flockmates for nearly an hour, before fading reluctantly away and taking the tom with her. I worried that my client would be disappointed, but he reacted as a true woodsman should, slapping me on the back and chortling about the wonder of seeing a wild creature up close. I loved every moment of it, too, but that hunt left me with as many questions as it did golden moments. For starters, why was the hen so fooled by the decoys, while the gobbler hung back, refusing to march in like his female companion? It's a good question; one that's not easily answered.

Ideally, decoys should work for turkey hunters like they do for waterfowlers; providing eye-candy for a bird whose ears have already been fooled. As many hunters know, a gobbler might come just so far to a call, then suddenly stop, stretch his neck and look for the source of his seduction. In many cases, if he doesn't see a hen, he puts on the brakes. Decoys are meant to solve such problems, and many times they do. Kill one swaggering longbeard that trudged the extra yards because he saw a fake hen, and you'll become a firm believer in decoys.

But sometimes decoys can create as many problems as they solve. The glitches can be minor, like a gobbler hanging just out of range or halting his death march as soon as he spots a decoy. Or decoy snafus can be major as when a big tom turns inside out when he encounters one. Even worse, decoys can create safety problems, putting a hunter in a dangerous situation that he wouldn't have experienced had he left his fakes at home.

As decoys become more available and their use more widespread, learning the downside of these hunting tools is as important as recognizing their value. For advice on this topic, I turned to three top turkey hunters: Tad Brown, call designer for M.A.D. Calls and a former hunting guide; Pat Reeve, videographer and pro staffer for Hunter's Specialties, Inc.; and Ron Gehrke, a veteran hunting guide from western Wisconsin and a member of the Outland Sports Gold Team. Their years of experience provide a clear picture of when decoys can work against you, and some ways that hunters can avoid unproductive or dangerous situations.

Spring into Action

Without hesitation, my trio of experts agree that decoys are most effective during early spring, before the breeding cycle hits its peak.

"That's when gobblers are still in bachelor groups and hens aren't ready for mating," Brown said. "There's intense competition between gobblers, and they can be

Decoy Deployment

Use decoys only where they're legal. Make sure to position them within shooting range of your location. Place the hen decoys facing away from you since gobblers want to approach hens from behind. Because gobblers will approach jakes from the front to fight, place the jake decoy (if you use one) facing toward you. To help conceal your position, try to keep some foliage between you and where you expect the gobbler to come from. Sit with your back to the base of a wide tree for safety.

Hen decoys
face away
from hunter

Expected
gobbler
routes

Jake decoy
faces hunter

easy to call and decoy. They remind me of white-tailed bucks during the pre-rut; chasing does around that want nothing to do with them. I've seen gobblers almost pile up on themselves when they encountered decoys—they seemed surprised that they were going to get close to a hen!"

As the breeding cycle progresses, gobbler response to decoys varies. "When breeding intensifies, getting gobblers to come to a decoy can be tough," Brown said. "Too many guys focus on the decoy and believe that the gobbler is suspicious of it, but that might not be true. During peak breeding, gobblers get so used to hens coming to them that they don't break like they do earlier in the season. If the bird gobbles and struts, but doesn't come, he might not necessarily be spooked; he's probably just stubborn. The hens have been coming to him and it hasn't clicked in his head that he might have to go to one in order to breed."

One solution to such a scenario is to place several decoys in a spread, rather than using a lone hen. "That works on two levels," Reeve said. "If the tom is with hens, for example, they might wander over to be with another group of birds. And if you have a jake or half-strut tom decoy in there, an older bird might get sucked in just out of dominance. I've even seen big gobblers leave hens to go over and run a jake or subordinate tom off."

Using decoys later in the season can be touchy business, according to the experts. "In the areas where I hunt, some of these toms have been hunted for six to seven weeks and have seen it all," Gerhke said. "Besides, breeding is winding down and the birds are tired; they just aren't going at it very hard. So I tone everything down, from the way that I call to the way that I put decoys out. I'd rather have 'em coming in looking than risk having a decoy out there that might put them off."

Can They Spot a Fake?

You can get good hunting camp discussions going by questioning how smart a turkey is. Some folks, with

lengthy observations about the oddball behavior of gobblers, will tell you that turkey gray matter is on par with spaghetti. Others, who've been repeatedly out-foxed by gobbler after gobbler, will tell you how unbelievably smart Ol' Tom is. Who's right? It depends on who's serving supper at turkey camp that night.

"I believe that gobblers learn from bad experiences," Reeve said. "In areas with high hunting pressure, you've got more guys bumping toms or shooting at long ranges as the turkeys come in to decoys. I think that mature toms learn to associate decoys with danger. This is especially true when using a single hen decoy with its head up. In the turkey's world, a bird standing like that is on alert and looking for danger. If she's not moving, the tom will be naturally cautious."

Brown agrees, and adds that fine-tuning a decoy setup can make a huge difference in how a gobbler reacts to it. "If I can, I like to partially obscure the gobbler's view of the decoys, maybe put them behind a little brush or partially behind a hill, so that he can't see everything. I think that increases the curiosity factor. It's like if you see a nice-looking girl across the room in plain view, you might be content to sit there and admire her. But if you get just a glimpse, you'll probably be tempted to walk over and check her out."

Perhaps the biggest trait of a decoy that reveals it as a fake is its inability to move. "That's one of the biggest drawbacks in my book," Gehrke said. "Decoys are 100 percent non-cooperative; they don't move or act like a turkey. The most obvious example is how still they sit. How often do you see live turkeys behave like that? Another thing is wind—you put a decoy out in a field on a windy day and it might move, but little of that movement looks anything like what a real turkey does."

Solutions to this glitch can vary in price and complexity. Brown likes to double-stake his decoys during a high wind, preventing them from spinning on their stakes or making erratic, unnatural movements. "Drive a second stake or a stick close to the base of the decoy's tail, and it won't make those crazy movements," he said. "In fact, the wind can add realism to the setup." Hunters can also use decoys that do move, or simply more realistic decoys, in their setups.

"There are several plastic and foam decoys on the market that allow you to move the head up and down by stringing a line to your position, and they're very effective," Reeve said. "I have a full-bodied mount of a hen turkey done by an award-winning taxidermist. The effect of those real feathers playing in a breeze is too much for most gobblers—they come right in. If you're serious and if it's legal in your area, you can even put motion in the decoys by having their heads bob. But now you're talking serious money and effort; at least $300 for the mount and a special carrying case to transport it in the field. It's more than I want to monkey with in most situations."

Do You Believe in Magic?

It sounds obvious, but for decoys to work you have to use them frequently and believe in them. Ron Gehrke is a case in point; the hard-working guide has seen a lot of clients wrap their tags around a gobbler's leg, but he admits to having little patience with decoys. "I'm a mobile hunter," he said. "If I think that I need to move and call a bird from a different location in order to kill it, I do so. I don't want to break down a field full of decoys. Besides, I've found that I like birds to come in looking for the hen that they heard. I've been able to get my clients more shot opportunities that way. Decoys kill a lot of birds and always will, but they don't suit my style of hunting most of the time."

While Tad Brown can cutt-'n'-run with the best of them, in most cases he prefers a slower test of wits between himself and a tom. "I like using decoys and discovering the calls a turkey will respond to that bring him into gun range," he said. "I enjoy watching a gobbler react to decoys, and if his reaction is negative, I try to learn from it. There's always another day and another gobbler to chase."

Reeve enjoys using dekes because they can turn gobblers into movie stars. "I tape turkey hunts all over the continent, and I want to milk the most out of every encounter that I get," he said. "When birds come to decoys, they display all those traits that make for a

When hunting with decoys, you put yourself at a higher risk in the field. Ensuring that you're equipped with hunter orange could prevent an unnecessary tragedy.

memorable, exciting hunt; strutting, gobbling, drumming, putting on a great show. Not just some bird piling into the call and getting shot."

Safety First

All three hunters agree that turkey hunting safety—already a red-letter topic of concern—becomes even more important when decoys are used. "Especially in public areas or farms where you know there are others hunting," Gehrke said. "We've all had close calls with decoys that might not have happened without them."

To prevent accidents while hunting with decoys, all three hunters urge others to carry decoys in hunter orange carrying sacks and to tie an orange tape or bandanna to the tree behind them when hunting in high-pressure areas. "I wouldn't hesitate to use those safety decoys with orange tail tips," Brown said. "I don't think that they spook birds, and they could prevent a tragedy." ❖

❖ Hunting in the Enchanted Land ❖

By Steve Bauer

As I sat with my back against the tree, I tried to block out the numbness that was rising through my legs. What I wouldn't give to shift them right now. Just a smidgen, anything to get the blood circulating down there again. I watched in agony as the gobbler fed lazily in the field toward us, not yet deciding if our hen calls were worthy of his investigation.

Suddenly, my cameraman for the hunt, Ronnie Strickland, broke the silence. "I've got enough footage, so when he steps inside 35 yards, go ahead and fire when you're ready." Optimistic words, I thought, considering that the tom had been hovering at about 40 yards for 10 minutes now. If he stayed there any longer, I was convinced that the numbness would soon work its way through my entire body, reducing me to a worthless heap of camouflage.

Then without warning, the tom broke into a strut, coming toward us with renewed vigor. The evening sun was the perfect backdrop for his magnificent show, the sunlight dancing off his feathers in a gorgeous display.

I was never so glad to have a cameraman at my back, and I hoped that the video would do justice to the scene in front of us. The tom quickly made his way inside 35 yards, and a soft putt put him at attention. I eased the safety off the Mossy Oak Break-Up camouflaged Winchester Model 1300, carefully lined up the sights and pulled the trigger. The tom hit the ground instantaneously.

I let out an embarrassing whoop of joy and rose to run to him, forgetting momentarily about my temporary paralysis. I didn't forget long, though, because when I attempted to put one foot in front of the other, a comedy of errors ensued. Not wanting to ruin the footage and look like a putz, I pushed ahead, trying to do my best impression of a run. It didn't work like I had hoped, however, and the best that I could manage with my dysfunctional legs was a fast waddle that resembled a wounded duck. The 30 yards to the tom seemed like it took days to cover, as I had to watch each leg move in front of the other to

ensure that I was still on my feet.

When I finally reached the bird, I was pleased at both the sensation heading back to my lower half and the beautiful, mature Merriam's gobbler lying at my feet. The shot had capped off a remarkable day of hunting, and I began to understand why they call New Mexico the "Land of Enchantment."

When I used to think of prime turkey habitat, New Mexico didn't come flooding to mind. I had always pictured the state as an arid, flat landscape that is home to wandering bands of pronghorns. And for much of the area, that's true. On the drive from Albuquerque to our camp east of Raton, pronghorns dotted the landscape in every direction, and the prominent color of the land was a depressing brown.

But once the elevation started increasing as we headed north, a new world emerged before our eyes. Mountainous terrain and pockets of thick timber and green fields screamed turkey habitat. As I surveyed the surroundings, I happily recalled that New Mexico allows hunters to take two birds during its spring season. For any turkey hunter who dreads ending the hunt too early with the pull of the trigger, the second tag is a great way to keep you out in the field longer. And with the turkey hunting possibilities abounding, I was never so glad to have an extra tag in my pocket.

Merriam's aren't as spooky as their Eastern cousins, but getting the gobblers to come to your calls can be like pulling teeth. Although the turkeys barely flinched when our trucks rumbled by, very few of the kills during the hunt were the result of gobblers running to hunters' setups. The hilly terrain made for weary toms, requiring a great deal of time spent face

The author poses with his second gobbler of the hunt. The mountainous terrain of northern New Mexico can pose a challenge for even the most experienced turkey hunter.

down in the grass, belly-crawling to try to get close enough for a shot. The decoys that we used were also met with limited success. On several occasions, I witnessed spooky hens lead gobblers away from our setup because of the presence of the decoys. But when it was all said and done, we must've been doing something right, because every member of the hunting group downed at least one gobbler. That's a success rate that no hunter can argue with.

During the last morning of our hunt, I barely had time to adjust myself into shooting position when a big gobbler flew down off his roost, 20 yards in front of me. As I lined up the shot, I laughed to myself at the fact that now that my legs were fully functional, there was no cameraman around to record this slam-dunk opportunity. After two days of hard hunting, however, it was fitting that this perfect New Mexico trip came down to a perfect setup. Once again, the 1300 made sure that the tom went down hard, and I was all smiles as I stood over my second gobbler in as many days. As I looked up at the brilliant pink and purple clouds streaking across the early morning sky, I had to admit: I, too, had become spellbound by the "Land of Enchantment." ❖

To begin gathering information for planning a New Mexico turkey hunt, contact the New Mexico Game and Fish Department at (505) 827-7911 or write them at:
New Mexico Game and Fish Department
Box 25112
Santa Fe, NM 87504
Visit their Web site at: www.gmfsh.state.nm.us/

❖ TARGETING FALL TOMS ❖

By Jim Spencer

Make no mistake: Hunting gobblers during the fall can be challenging. They aren't interested in mating at this time of year, so their survival instinct doesn't get drowned out by testosterone, making them warier.

Still, there are ways to seek out, hunt and kill gobblers during the fall. It just takes more work than it does during the spring. Basically, there are two fall hunting philosophies—hunt conservatively or pull out all the stops.

Spring tactics, such as aggressively calling to gobblers, can work in the fall, too.

The Conservative Approach

"Successfully hunting fall gobblers is 99 percent scouting," said John Vaca, a veteran fall gobbler chaser from northwest Missouri. During the fall, Vaca says that turkeys are concerned with three things: feeding, flocking and survival. Their breeding instinct lies dormant until spring triggers the annual mating ritual.

"Fall hunting is a different type of hunting from spring, when the turkeys are running around with sex on the brain," Vaca said. "Hunters try to take advantage of that during the spring, but you can't use that trick during the fall."

Vaca says that he likes to scout for two to three weeks prior to the fall season to pattern the movements of turkeys in the area. He attempts to see the turkeys, but tries not to spook them in the process. He does a lot of sitting, watching and listening.

"They're usually not as vocal during the fall, but they're still there," he said. "By knowing their habits, you can set up an ambush between Point A and Point B. Hunt all day during the fall; you might make contact with turkeys at any time. Since fall gobblers usually roost in the same area every night, if you aren't successful during the day you can set up near the roost and hunt them as they come back in the afternoon."

Vaca says that breaking up a flock of mature birds and calling them back in is another good way to hunt fall gobblers—although he admits that it requires more patience than breaking up a flock of young turkeys and doing the same thing.

"When you break up a flock of gobblers, watch closely as they disperse," he advises. "If you see a good gobbler go in a particular direction, go that way before you set up. If you set up in the direction that you see a particular gobbler run or fly away, you'll have a better chance at that bird."

Knowing the lay of the land is also helpful when targeting fall toms. "Turkeys take the easy route when they're not being pressured," he said. "Use natural

Artwork by Jim Kasper. Courtesy of the artist and Wild Wing's, Inc., Lake City, Minnesota.

Generally, turkeys aren't as vocal in the fall, but they will gobble and respond to other turkey vocalizations if the mood hits them.

bottlenecks and funnels such as saddles, forest roads and ridges to your advantage.

"Nothing is 100 percent effective, spring or fall," Vaca said. "But the more you know about the habits of the turkeys that you're hunting during the fall, the better off you'll be."

Autumn Acts of Aggression

Brad Harris, vice president of public relations for Outland Sports and one of the most successful turkey hunters in the business, agrees with Vaca's philosophy for hunting fall gobblers—to a point.

"There are two ways to hunt fall gobblers—conservatively or aggressively," Harris said. "The conservative approach is effective, and for a long time I believed that was the only way to hunt them. Bushwhacking, stalking, calling softly and sparingly are part of the conservative style of hunting. But over the past few years, I've begun to notice a change in the behavior of fall turkeys, and I've modified my hunting techniques to take advantage of it."

Harris says that when he was a youngster hunting deer and other game in the hills and hollows of the eastern Ozarks, it was rare to hear a turkey gobble during the fall. Nowadays, he says that he hears them all the time, and often they gobble as aggressively as they do during the spring. He says that other hunters are telling him the same thing.

"I don't know the reason, but I suspect that it's partly due to the fact that we have higher turkey densities in many areas than we've ever had before," Harris said. "Fall turkeys aren't very vocal on bad-weather days, but when the weather is mild, they can really crank it up."

Harris says that he lets the weather du jour dictate his hunting tactics for fall gobblers. On cloudy, windy, cold days, he falls back on the traditional, conservative tactics described by Vaca, doing a lot of slipping along and looking for turkeys; calling softly, being patient and stealthy. But when the day is nice, he gets unconventional. And it works.

"In bluebird weather, I've found that it's productive to get aggressive with fall gobblers," Harris said. "I call to 'em just like it was spring, with locator calls, loud, fast hen yelps, cutts, gobbles, fighting calls, gobbler yelps; you name it. I try to cover as much ground as possible, just like I do during the spring, looking for a gobbler or group of gobblers that want to play."

"Play," however, is probably an inaccurate word to use in this context. Harris believes that, to an extent, turkeys are susceptible to the same social pressures that humans are. In higher population densities, turkeys, become more ... well, for lack of a better term, irritable. Too many beings crammed into too little available space causes friction, and friction leads to open conflict. It's why you read about a high incidence of road rage on the Los Angeles freeway system, but rarely hear of any overt driver aggression in Tiptonville, Tennessee.

It's Harris's contention that the increasing turkey population density in many areas of the country—his home state of Missouri, for example, and in neighboring eastern Kansas—is causing gobblers to become more aggressive toward each other. Turkeys aren't exactly territorial, but Harris believes that they still get grumpier with each other as population densities continue to increase.

"In the past two or three years, I've learned that this loud, aggressive stuff works," he said. "We're making longbeards come in gobbling and strutting, just like they do during the spring. Surely it's not a breeding impulse that's causing them to do this—it's bound to be tied to dominance—but whatever it is, it's happening more."

The Dominance Factor

Harris has long believed that dominance is more important in dictating turkey behavior than the breeding instinct.

"The turkey breeding season lasts only a few weeks," he said, "but the struggle for dominance goes on all year. It never stops and it's present in all segments of the turkey population. Adult gobblers have a pecking order, and so do immature gobblers. Hens do, too. And these pecking orders are constantly changing."

Harris says that even during spring, when turkeys are in a fizz over the mating season, dominance overrides the breeding instinct.

"That's why a big gobbler will face off with a jake decoy rather than going directly to a hen decoy when you have a mixed decoy spread," he said. "For the moment, at least, the gobbler is more interested in establishing his

dominance over the jake than he is in servicing the hen."

Harris says that although he hasn't been doing it long enough to be absolutely sure of what's happening, he believes that it's easier to fire a turkey up during the fall where turkey densities are high.

"The gobblers are bunched up during this time of year, but there are getting to be more bunches of them," Harris said. "That makes them not only easier to find, but it also makes it easier to fool them into thinking that their dominance is being challenged. It's getting easier to set 'em off."

Harris says that he hasn't abandoned the tactic of breaking up a flock of gobblers and calling them back, but he has specific ideas about the timing of this tactic.

"If you're going to bust up a bunch of gobblers, do it late in the afternoon or even after they've flown up," he advises. "It's much more difficult to get a wide dispersal when you're breaking up a gobbler flock during the day, and it takes a lot longer for a bunch of old birds to get back together in full daylight. But when you break them up late in the day, they won't be able to find each other before dark and each of them will have to spend the night alone. The next morning, if you get out there among the scattered gobblers, you can call them back much easier." Harris says that he uses a lot of coarse gobbler clucks for this, but has also had success by staging a gobbler fight.

"We're in the heyday of turkey hunting," Harris said. "Nationwide, it's never been better. You probably need a pretty good turkey population to make these aggressive tactics work, but so far I've seen them work in Texas, Missouri and Kansas, and they'll work in other states, too."

So if you've been lukewarm about hunting turkeys during the fall because young birds aren't your thing and fall gobblers are too tough, maybe you ought to give Harris's aggressive tactics a try on your hunting grounds. If they don't work, you can always take a page out of the traditional tactics playbook and hunt like Vaca advocates.

If you feel silly out there cutting and cackling when the trees are losing their leaves instead of growing them, take a look on the bright side: Who's gonna see you? ❖

❖ SCATTERING STRATEGIES FOR FALL ❖

By Glenn Sapir

Because calling to undisturbed turkeys is not as dependable during the fall as it is during the spring, fall turkey hunters must use different strategies to be successful. The most popular fall turkey hunting technique involves finding a flock of birds, scattering them and then taking advantage of their desire to reassemble.

Before you can scatter a flock of birds, however, you must first locate them. Knowing their preferred food sources is a great start. But according to Bill Hollister, a retired wildlife biologist and avid turkey hunter, putting on some miles by foot can increase your odds of finding the birds before they find you. "Using the contours of the land that you're hunting will allow you to sneak in close enough to the birds to get a good scatter and it might even allow you to get a shot before they break up," he said.

"The best scatters occur when you get almost the entire flock airborne," Hollister said. "If some birds run off in the same direction, that's okay, as long as others fly or run in opposite directions. Getting all the birds to scatter in different directions doesn't happen often."

Post-Scatter Setup

During fall, hunting strategies are different than during spring, but you still have to call the birds. In this situation, the hunter scatters the turkeys at point A, hoping to get them flying off in different directions. The hunter then has two options: set up near the point where the scatter occurred, or head uphill 50 to 100 yards to a strategic setup spot to start calling the birds back (B). Why set up uphill from the scatter point? Because often turkeys, especially wary adult toms, will circle around and uphill, trying to come from above and descend on the scatter point as they re-group—

Setting Up

Once you have the birds scattered, you need to figure out where to set up and you also should have a handle on what calls to use and when. If you can scatter the turkeys in different directions, chances are good that they—especially hens and poults—will attempt to reassemble close to the point where they were initially dispersed.

"If the birds scatter by fanning out, sometimes they'll get back together at an assembly point near the area where they flew," Hollister said. "If you scatter gobblers, they'll usually reassemble by approaching the scatter point from a higher elevation so that they can

Field

KEY
─Scattering Turkeys
─Returning Turkeys
A─Scatter Point
B─Setup Point

Ridge

possibly in an attempt to see if the danger that flushed them is still there. And your calls will project farther if you're higher in elevation.

observe the area that they were scattered from."

Hens with poults might attempt to reassemble within minutes of the scatter. Gobblers, however, can take hours to reassemble. Hollister will use this time to select a comfortable setup that he thinks will present a good shot. He'll often set up a portable ground blind, creating further concealment.

After Hollister is in position, he waits for the turkeys to begin calling. "If you're dealing with hens and poults, you should use assembly yelps and kee-kee runs—the high-pitched whistling of an immature bird—to try to get the birds to come to you. With gobblers, you should use coarse clucks and yelps with a slower cadence than those that you would expect to hear from hens."

Sometimes the flock will not have such distinct sex divisions. "Often, late during the season, especially if you have snow on the ground, you might get mixed flocks of adult gobblers, hens and poults," Hollister said. "When you break up a mixed flock of turkeys, the hens and poults will usually reassemble first. But a couple of years ago, I had just the opposite occur. After scattering a mixed flock, the first bird to come back in was a gobbler and the next was a hen. The poults hadn't even sounded off yet. So you can't always go by the book."

Fall Turkey Patterns

Familiarizing yourself with the day-to-day patterns of turkeys during the fall can be a great way to locate them when the hunting season starts.

"It's good to be in the woods at dusk during the fall," Hollister said. "If you're quiet, you can often hear turkeys fly up into their roosting trees. If you can scatter them off the roost at dusk, even if they fly only 50 yards to a different tree, they'll want to get back together in the morning. They'll often be so eager to get back together that they'll start calling right after fly-down. Sit at the location where you scattered them, and you could have the birds come in without having to call."

Hollister suggests relying on others to help you locate turkeys during the fall. "Rural letter carriers and school bus drivers are good scouts," he said. "So are bowhunters, who'll be in their treestands or ground blinds until dark and might see or hear turkeys fly up on roost. This information could lead to a great morn-

ing hunt ... if you don't mind being called at home in the middle of the night." There are some inconveniences that are worth putting up with when it comes to successfully hunting turkeys during the fall. ❖

Wisconsin hunter Pat Krieger with his first turkey—a young hen called up by NAHC editor Tom Carpenter, after a classic scatter.

❖ Fall Turkeys the Other Way ❖

By Tom Carpenter

Fall turkey hunting enchants me. But the time-honored and traditional scatter-and-call-'em-back technique presents a logistical problem.

As a regular guy, my main fall turkey hunting territory consists of only two hill-country farms. If I scatter the resident birds, I might have just done one of the following things: pushed my quarry onto land that I can't hunt; sent the birds over there for good; or spooked my season's available quarry.

Maybe you only have access to limited land, too, or are looking for a more laid-back approach to fall turkey hunting. The following low-impact hunting strategies will leave the turkeys how you want them: calm and confident. And where you want them: on land that you can hunt.

Scouting Is Key

Scout during summer and early fall. Know where the turkeys roost, feed, dust, get water and grit and "hang out." Walk the woods and fields looking for sign. Watch and glass for moving turkeys. Use this scouting knowledge when you put the following hunting strategies to work.

Hunt the Roost—Dawn

If you have an idea where turkeys are roosting (or better yet, actually saw them fly up), sneak in close before first light the next morning and set up. As fly-down time nears, call with soft clucks and yelps. Try to lure the birds your way after they fly down. It helps to be between the roost and where the turkeys want to go.

Morning Setups

After the sun rises, set up near feeding areas—the corner of a harvested grain field is great, as are meadows. Or set up where you've seen turkeys traveling, or at spots where they're likely to pass: a point of timber, along a fenceline, beside a finger of brush or in a funnel area between woods, fields or hills.

Put out a decoy or two to give visual assurance to incoming turkeys or to attract the attention of birds that don't hear your calls. Make purrs and clucks. Belt out a few lonely yelps every so often. Turkeys like company during the fall and will often check out any newcomers (your decoys) to the territory.

Spot & Get Ahead

Spot and observe turkeys from a strategic vantage point and try to determine their travel route. Sneak ahead of the birds and set up. Put out some decoys, get comfortable and make a few soft yelps. Don't call non-stop, but purr and cluck a little between yelps. Wait at least an hour for extra-pokey birds.

Afternoon Setups

Hunt in the "hanging out" cover that you scouted. Stay in your setups for an hour or so, at strategic spots in the woods or along field edges. Call with soft purrs and clucks. Yelp occasionally.

If the weather is unseasonably warm, go to an area with spring seeps or other dampness. If it's windy, head for calmer areas on the lee side of hills and in hollows. Woods with hard mast are good in the afternoon. Overgrown or fallow fields are also great places to hunt.

Sneak-and-Yelp

The "sneak-and-yelp," fall's answer to spring's "cutt-and-run," is essentially a still-hunt through good turkey territory.

Move slowly and quietly. Attempt to spot turkeys before they spot you. Stop often to call. Call blind at strategic spots as you go. Stroke, scratch or blow out a few yelps. Kee-kees are effective, too. Sooner or later you'll get an answer. Always be ready to set up quickly; forget about decoys, the turkeys might already be on their way.

Hunt the Roost—Evening

Sneak into a roost area at least an hour before sunset, set up quietly with a couple of decoys out and wait for the birds. Purr and cluck lightly—like you're an early bird already in the bedroom and everything is safe.

Don't call too loudly or aggressively. In the calm of an evening, your soft little mumbles, whines and purrs will be plenty loud.

Calls for Fall

Turkeys are vocal and gregarious during the fall, and calling need not be complex. Yelps are essential; put some emotion into them, as if to say, "I'm lost," "I'm lonely" or "Where are you?" Kee-kees—the "lost" calls of young birds—will bring in both juveniles and mature birds. Purrs and clucks are important at your setups—the sounds of safe, contented turkeys. Scratch a few leaves like a feeding turkey would. ❖

Autumn's Finest Prize

Last fall I spotted a group of feeding turkeys, looped ahead of them, climbed the low oak ridge and set up. Nothing happened for a long time, but I was very happy with a couple decoys out, October's sun warming my bones, and autumn's woods ablaze with color around me.

And then some soft yelps answered my plaintive calling. I perked up, adjusted my facemask, got the shotgun set, picked up the box and called again. Yelps replied from half the distance! I laid the box down and waited, my heart pounding as hard as it ever could.

At 18 yards, a good bird stepped into an opening (in fall, any turkey is a good turkey), and the gorgeous adult hen folded at the shot. I limped over on stiff legs, a happy man, to claim autumn's finest prize.

Low-impact hunting might be the best method if you have a limited amount of land to hunt.

BIRDS, BUNNIES & MORE

With hunting, even small game can create big excitement. Watch a seasoned shooter fall to pieces when a 1½ pound ruffed grouse explodes at his feet, or a covey of quail (weighing in at a whopping 8 ounces each) whirls up from the grass. Feel your heart pick up the pace when the hounds turn the corner, and you know a cottontail is on its way back to you and could emerge from the raspberry brambles at any moment. Look at the wide eyes of a duck hunter hunkered in a blind as the birds set their wings to come on in.

Yes, birds of all kinds—and bunnies—stir fervent and loyal hunting emotions. You might even try hunting the hunters themselves—predators such as coyotes, foxes and bobcats—to add extra time and excitement to your hunting year.

❖ BEAGLE BEGINNINGS ❖

By Brad Harris

When it comes to excitement and commitment to the task at hand, nothing performs as enthusiastically as a beagle in pursuit of a briar rabbit. Most beagles will run or pursue rabbits, but there is a big difference between chasing rabbits and running them with style, control and consistency. All the pieces of the puzzle must be in place to produce a complete rabbit dog.

Every hunter has his or her ideas of what qualities a rabbit dog should have. A rabbit dog does not have to be registered to be a good dog. As a matter of fact, I have owned registered dogs and grade dogs on both ends of the rabbit dog spectrum. The bad ones usually don't stay around long regardless of their backgrounds. My dad always said that it takes just as much money to feed a good dog as it does a bad one. I look for a dog with a good nose that has the ability to run scents in different weather and ground conditions. A desire to hunt is evident in dogs that live to pursue aggressively with enthusiasm, drive and determination.

I also want a dog that has good rabbit sense. This characteristic has a wide range of interpretation. I look for a dog that runs within its ability and only pursues rabbits. Nothing ruins a hunt faster than a trashy hound.

A dog should have enough sense to slow down when scenting conditions are bad and speed up when they're good. A good dog is not overly mouthy—barking for no reason or whenever it is unsure. When a rabbit dog opens, there should be a rabbit in front of it. When it does open for the right reasons, I want to hear a lot of noise. There are hundreds of different traits that you could look for in a dog, but these are the ones that I want and demand: speed, conformation, color and size. Whether a dog is male or female is a personal preference. The first thing that you must do is to be selective in what you start with.

If you have purchased a started hound with the above characteristics, all you need to do is put it in the field and give it the running time necessary to hone its skills. If you start with a puppy, remember that training begins at birth. Spending time with a new dog every day is a critical step in developing a bond. Play with your puppies and let children and others join in as well.

By working your young beagles with more experienced dogs, the pups quickly learn the ins and outs of hunting rabbits.

Let puppies be puppies, but also make sure that they know you are in control. Get them used to coming to you when you call; name them early and then use their name often to let them know who they are. Call to them at feeding time. They will soon begin to recognize your voice and associate it with something good. Make noise around them, bang feed bowls together and then watch their response and reassure them if they become frightened. Do this gradually to prepare them for future hunts when a shotgun comes into play.

I take my beagles to the field when they're 6 to 7 months old. Short trips are best. Don't wear them out and always stay within eyesight of them. Move into brush with the pups and encourage them to explore. After a few outings, they will become bolder and more inquisitive. It's at this time that I try to get them into rabbits on a regular basis.

When a rabbit is jumped or located, call to the dogs with excitement, pointing and showing them where it came from and what direction it traveled. Let them smell a fresh rabbit bed, and show them that you are excited about it as well. From day one, when I jump a rabbit I scream, "Wee! Wee! Wee!" as loud and as high-pitched as I can. The dogs soon recognize this as a signal that a rabbit has been jumped and they will come running. Some people use "Tally Ho!" but I can't get high enough or sound excited enough with this phrase.

Whatever sound you use, start with it from the beginning stages of training and stick with it. A beagle has a burning desire to please its master, and if its master is excited about something, the dog will be, too. After your dog starts trailing on its own, it's up to you to keep it interested in rabbits.

Spending time afield is the best way to continue your dog's development. Encourage him and never let him quit. If he comes back to you, take him to the point where he quit and then push him to continue.

Another way to jump-start a pup is to use domesticated rabbits. The San Juan breed resembles cottontails in scent and appearance. Turn one out and let a 3- to 5-month-old puppy give chase. This does a lot to boost a pup's desire to pursue. Generally, the rabbit will run a short distance and then give out, letting the pup catch it.

Keep in mind that no two dogs develop at the same

Beagles learn by spending time in the field hunting. The more time you spend in the woods with your hounds, the more polished their skills will be.

pace. Some start out fast, some slow, yet it takes time to develop any hound into a good gun dog. I don't worry about where a dog starts, but where it finishes. Gun over them for two hunting seasons before you pass judgment. Let young dogs learn at their own pace. Do not hunt them with older dogs until you are sure that they can physically keep up, and then only run them for short periods of time. Don't burn them out. Never run young dogs with old ones that have bad habits. I would rather run a dog by itself than ruin it by running it with a dog that does a poor job of chasing rabbits.

Training a beagle takes patience, dedication and persistence. Eventually, when it all comes together, it's pure joy listening to and watching your gun dog do it right. ❖

❖ BOWS & BUNNIES ❖
By Gordy Krahn

My heart raced as a ribbon of downy fur weaved through a tangled snarl of tag alders and red willows. Hare one second ... gone the next. I lowered my bow—raised it again as I caught a glimpse of frosty-white bunny butt crossing a scant trail 15 yards in front of me—lowered it as it vanished in the blink of an eye.

"Coming your way!" Bill Marchel yelled from behind a stringy wall of young aspens. "He's headed for that blow-down." Bill had cut off the hare's escape and it was circling back toward me.

I dropped to my knees, hoping to purchase a better view. Sure enough, there they were; two small, black saucers, gleaming like polished coals against the snowy backdrop. It's their eyes that always give them away.

I hurriedly nocked an arrow and, still on my knees, drew back my bow and quickly stroked the release. I cursed under my breath as a wispy aspen whipped from side to side, sending the arrow sharply off-target. The bunny was gone in half a heartbeat.

"Did you get him?" Bill ran to the blow-down and habitually began looking for any sign of a hit.

"Don't think so," I joined him. "Shooting through this brush is like trying to thread a needle with mittens on."

Lindy Frasl and Vince Meyer were waiting on the edge of a clear-cut where they were serving as blockers for our mini bunny-drive. They had joined Bill and me on the chilly February morning hunt in northern Minnesota.

"There was another one to the right of you," Vince pointed at a dim trail barely visible in the thick under-brush. "He saw us before we could shoot and then doubled back around you."

Bill took the lead, plowing through the shin-high snow. "Let's push that patch next to the road," he called back. "We jumped a couple of rabbits there the other week and didn't get either of them."

When I was a kid growing up in northern Minnesota, bush rabbits, as we called them, were as

Hunting hares with a bow is as challenging as small game hunting gets. And the amount of fun you'll have will make up for all those lost arrows.

common as crows. Rarely did you set foot in the woods without seeing several. Varying hares, so named because their furred coats change from their gray-brown of summer to almost pure white by mid-winter are, in fact, common throughout most of Canada and the northern United States.

When my brother, Tony, and I hunted hares back in the early 1970s, our success was usually measured in large body counts. It was relatively easy to shoot a limit with a shotgun or a .22 rimfire rifle or handgun. By mid-decade, however, hare numbers had dropped off drastically and, for whatever reason, failed to recover.

There are still hares in some of my old haunts, but not nearly as many.

Fluctuations in hare populations are well-documented, and can be traced back more than 200 years in the fur records of the Hudson's Bay Company. The interval between successive peaks averages about 10 years. During population peaks, hares often become extremely abundant and have historically coincided with the turn of each decade throughout their range.

Hares occupy fairly small territories and are some-what nocturnal. During the day, they rest in sheltered areas beneath snow-laden evergreen branches or blow-downs, where they doze or groom themselves.

During these rest periods, hares also excrete and then eat soft, green pellets of partially digested food. In much the same way that a cow or sheep chews and digests its food twice, these pellets go back into the hare's digestive chamber, where additional nutrients are extracted before the hard, fully digested pellets are eliminated.

Snow-packed trails are common where hare popula-tions are high. These are frequently used by the resident hares as they travel between feeding and resting areas.

Hares use two basic strategies to evade their ene-mies: hiding and fleeing. Large eyes set high on their heads allow them to see in nearly all directions, while long ears swivel independently to pick up sounds. As long as they're undetected, hares remain still, hoping that predators will pass by.

Once discovered, however, they leap from cover and use their incredible agility and speed to escape. They will typically travel in a large circular route that keeps them within the relative safety of their territory, which they know intimately.

Tony and I generally flank each other, about 30 to 40 yards apart, and walk slowly, stopping to survey the woods every few steps, much like you would still-hunt for whitetails. Often, we will spot a hare in its bed and then make the shot. Or, if we jump one, it frequently runs only a short distance before stopping to look back.

I also use this method when hunting alone. By mov-ing slowly and quietly, I seldom spook hares badly and am often offered a stationary or slow-moving target.

If you are hunting with two or more partners, a bunny-drive is the way to go. Fan out in a straight line about 20 or 30 yards apart and walk slowly through the woods. Try to select small islands of cover that you can span and have a hunter flank each edge where the brush meets open cover. Hares like to skirt the edge of the cover as they double back.

When you near the end of the drive, have two hunters to one side hold up, positioned on trails. The other pushers should continue on and then veer in the direction of the stationary hunters and push back toward them, hoping to trap the hares in the middle. This worked well on several occasions during our February hunt, but you can expect the bunnies to panic at some point, and the action can be fast and furious; a difficult scenario if you're hunting with archery tackle.

Hunting snowshoe hares with stick and string is a low-percentage game at best. But if you're up to the challenge, and aren't counting on rabbit stew for sup-per, it's a good way to sharpen your hunting and shooting skills in the off-season. I had gone through my gear the night prior to the hunt and selected arrows and broadheads that were far from pristine. I knew that an arrow released was likely an arrow lost. I decided to go with the same broadheads that I had used for target practice prior to and during deer sea-son, since my bow was already set up for them.

Most shots are within 30 yards and any tip, including field tips, judo points and broadheads, will kill these small animals. Practice drawing and quickly releasing arrows so that you are prepared for the fast action.

Our half-day hunt was coming to a close. We had made several small drives and never failed to move at least one hare, and sometimes we jumped three or four in a single push. My quiver was six arrows light and my nerves were shot. The rest of the crew had had equal luck; everyone had flung arrows without a hit.

I was flanking the edge of a swamp on our final drive and looked up to see a hare running up a trail directly at me. Surprised, I nocked an arrow and drew as it skidded to a halt, weighing its options for escape. This time I had a clear shot and did not waste the opportunity. The arrow found its mark and we had our first and only hare of the day.

It was time to call it a hunt. I was tired as I joined my friends for the walk back to the truck. What a great way to spend a cold winter day. ❖

❖ COTTONTAILS: A LOST TRADITION ❖

By John Sloan

A cold January wind rustled the broad palmetto leaves, and the Spanish moss swayed in the branches of the cypress and tupelo gums. I gripped the stock of my single-shot 20 gauge a little tighter and kicked a brush pile. That's all it took. The rabbit made a break for home and Mother, but my No. 6s caught up. I was 10, and that was my first cottontail. That began a love affair with bunnies that has lasted for many years.

In the South, rabbits were once a main staple for young hunters. Still-hunting for brush bunnies was a way of life. The season was long and the bag limit was liberal, and most farmers would grant permission to hunt. This was a training ground for still-hunting and safe gun handling. Young hunters learned quickly that shooting in the direction of another hunter was grounds for loss of hunting privileges.

Rabbit hunting was cheap. A shotgun and a few shotshells were all that you needed. When I was a youngster, the walk to the store was about a half-mile. Shotgun shells were a nickel each. I could pick up enough pop bottles at two cents each to buy three or four shells, and I would then hunt my way home, walking through the neighbors' fields. It was a learning experience. If you only have a few shells, you don't waste shots. Fortunately, my family never had to depend on my hunting abilities for food, but we ate what I killed, and rabbits were a favorite meal.

There are several effective methods for hunting cottontails. True, following a pack of beagles in full cry is a heart-thumping experience. I have owned and run beagles and love it. But there is something about the stalk, the sneak and the strategy of still-hunting rabbits that intrigues me.

Spot-and-Stalk

I break still-hunting for bunnies down into three methods: spot-and-stalk, stomp-and-flush and drive-and-kick. Of the three, I prefer a spot-and-stalk hunt with my old, single-shot .22 rifle. Spot-and-stalk

hunting isn't difficult, but it requires skill and patience. First, you must learn where rabbits are most likely to hide. Brush piles are a safe bet, as are old, fallen-in buildings. Briar tangles, though tough to see into, are also excellent. Most experienced hunters will tell you to look for the eyes and that's pretty good advice, because they shine and will give a rabbit away.

Once you spot a rabbit, if it's close enough, shoot. If not, plan a careful stalk. Rabbits, much like white-tailed deer, will often let you walk by if they think that they are hidden. Ignore the rabbit and take a circuitous route that will afford you a shot. If you really want to have some fun, try stalking rabbits with archery equipment.

Stomp-and-Flush

When stomp-and-flush hunting, I carry my 20 gauge loaded with No. 6 shot. Stomp-and-flush hunting is just what the name implies. You stomp on every brush pile and briar tangle that you encounter, with the goal of flushing a rabbit and making the shot. As with spot-and-stalk, this method can be done alone or with a hunting partner.

Drive-and-Kick

The drive-and-kick method works best for party hunts. This style of hunting dictates that a shotgun or archery equipment is used. Hunters line up in a straight line, a safe shooting distance apart, and then

walk through fields and other prime rabbit cover. The idea is to "kick" a rabbit up and flush it to where someone has a shot. These types of hunts are fun because they provide great exercise and a cure for "cabin fever."

While hunting in my home state of Tennessee, I once found a bunch of bunnies that would venture into an old garden plot just before dark each night. Some evenings there would be as many as 10. I suppose that they were feeding on the fertilized grass and weeds that had grown to cover the spot. I sneaked in one evening and rested my trusty .22 across an old stump hidden by weeds. I shot five rabbits with five shots. That's the only time that I've hunted rabbits from a ground blind.

The Disappearing Bunny

So the 10-year-old boy grew up, left the swamp and traveled to many states. By then, my hunting education was well in hand and I had moved on to other game: whitetails, mule deer, elk, turkeys, caribou and all sorts of other critters. And then one day it occurred to me that I hadn't seen many rabbits lately. It was once common to see four or five cottontails in my backyard every evening, but I haven't seen one there in two years. And I'm not alone.

An old rabbit-hunting friend of mine has a theory about what has happened. When I asked him where the cottontails had gone, he said, "Somewhere where they ain't cleaned out all the fencerows and sprayed everything with poison."

My friend might be right. He is much older and probably wiser than me, but that's too easy of an answer. I think that it's a combination of things.

Pesticides, herbicides and other chemicals have probably contributed to the decline in rabbit numbers. And many biologists will tell you that increasing predator populations have impacted rabbit populations. A decline in the fur market has fox, coyote and raccoon populations at record highs in many areas. Hawks get their share, too, and there seems to be more of them around today than ever before.

Waning Interest

There also seems to be a decreased interest in hunting rabbits. In many cases, white-tailed deer, which are now abundant across most of North America, have replaced rabbits as a training tool for young hunters. Where deer were once scarce, they now outnumber rabbits.

Add to this a lack of organized sportsmen's groups to champion the preservation of rabbit habitat, which has led to a decrease in environments where rabbits thrive. Show me an area where rabbits are still a major species and I'll show you an area with good rabbit habitat. But as to which causes which, I don't know.

And as houses and shopping centers replace farm fields, and more people move to cities and raise their children, the decrease in rabbit hunting grows. There is very little money in rabbit hunting. There are no great lodges booking rabbit hunts; no camo manufacturer is promoting a new rabbit pattern; no farm kid is dependent on his single barrel and two shells to provide the evening meal.

Rabbit hunting, as it used to be, might be a thing of the past. It is becoming a lost tradition. Only in areas where short deer seasons and a scarcity of other game exist, does rabbit hunting still hold on. And that's a shame, because it is sad to lose such a valuable tradition and a fun and challenging activity for young and old hunters alike. ❖

❖ STRATEGIES FOR SPRING SNOWS ❖

By Bill Miller

Spring snow geese are different birds than you have hunted in the fall. It might not seem possible, but they are even more fickle on the move north than they were on their way south! The keys to success in February, March and April revolve around being mobile and keeping an open mind about new ways to hunt geese.

Electronic Calling

When the use of electronic callers was legalized for the spring seasons, most dedicated snow goose hunters

believed that it would work well for a couple of seasons until the birds figured it out. It didn't last that long! While the tapes, or better yet, compact discs, of recorded live birds are definitely worthwhile investments, don't think that they'll have birds dropping in like long-lost kin! You still have to do everything else right, and the birds still have to be in the mood for company.

Carry several different tapes from different call companies. If one's not working, try a different recording. Equip each hunter with a caller and try combining dif-

A sight to both behold and beware. Snow goose hunting opportunities have never been better because snows have never been more over-populated.

ferent recordings played at the same time. You have to find a sound that those birds haven't heard just prior to being shot at.

If calling fails, try being quiet. This is especially true when dealing with huge flocks of birds. I've hunted with as many as six electronic callers all going on high volume, and when 1,000 or more birds are overhead, I still have doubts about whether the geese can hear anything but themselves.

Decoy Differently

In spring hunting, there are no juvenile birds. In the last decade, those few young birds in the fall flocks are what snow goose hunters have come to rely on for success. In the spring flocks, every one of these birds has seen decoy spreads, been called to and experienced gunfire. They've been hunted pretty much every day since leaving the nesting grounds early last September. Talk about spooky!

It seems that the birds recognize most decoy spreads from a long way off, but there's still something about a huge white spread that will at least get their attention and entice them to look—even if it's from 300 or 400 yards away. If birds are flaring from your spread, get away from it. Use it to hold their attention while you camouflage yourself in their flight path a quarter- or even half-mile away. It's pass-shooting, but at least it's shooting.

Consummate Camouflage

Because the birds are so wary, perfect camouflage is essential. Face masks or face paint is definitely in order. Blinds like the Final Approach that offer total concealment are necessary even if you're hunting from a spread. The birds are so fickle, however, and traveling so much in the spring, that digging "permanent" pits is usually a waste of time.

Hunters in the Dakotas have had some good success with both commercial and homemade round hay bale blinds. Twin plywood cutouts of cattle mounted on four bicycle wheels complete with gun racks on the inside have also been useful for spring snow goosers. These specialized, hand-built rigs can be used either as a blind near a decoy spread or as a way to sneak up on a feeding flock of birds to jump-shoot them.

Spring snow goose action can be fast and furious.

Use the Wind

Strong winds can be your best ally when hunting spring snows. In heavy winds, the birds will generally travel shorter distances from resting and roosting areas to feeding fields. They'll also tend to fly at lower altitudes. If the weather forecast calls for strong winds, find a flock of roosted birds, then try to figure out which direction they'll go to feed and get permission to set up in the flight path.

If you guess wrong, don't just "sit it out." Make the necessary moves to get under the flying birds as close to their roost as possible. Again, it's not decoy shooting, but it is shooting.

Not only are snow geese devastating their arctic habitat, they can ravage agricultural crops during their migration.

Heavyweight Champions

If you do get shooting at spring snows, it almost certainly will be at maximum effective ranges and under extremely windy conditions.

These are the times for which 3½-inch 10 gauge and 3½-inch 12 gauge magnums were created. Tungsten and bismuth-loaded shells are the best choices in non-toxics under these extreme conditions. (See "Long-Distance Goose Loads," next column.)

Chokes should be the tightest that will still handle these loads. Try modified for tungsten and light full for bismuth. Swing hard, get ahead of the birds and try to put the center of the load well forward on the goose. Head and neck shots kill the surest.

Mud, Mud, Mud

You've got to be a "mudder" to succeed in spring snow goosing. Generally, you're hunting in harvested

Long-Distance Goose Loads

Any waterfowler planning to undertake the time, expense and challenge of setting up on spring snow geese deserves to be properly armed. If ever there was a time to shell out the greenbacks for some spendy shotshells, this would be it.

With a penchant for taunting hunters from 50 to 60 yards, and then flying off to some other field, snow geese are generally safe from swarms of steel. Enter non-toxic alternatives like bismuth and tungsten. Federal's tungsten-iron loads have proven their worth in goose fields across North America during the past couple of seasons—even at nearly $2 per shell.

A new federally approved option on the market is Hevi-Shot, a tungsten-nickel-iron combination load that is reportedly even more dense (12 grams per cubic centimeter) than the other tungsten shot (10 g/cc) on the market. This density makes it even heavier than lead. In fact, on the company's Web site, www.hevi-shot.com, you can find a number of charts that compare the performance of Hevi-Shot to its competitors.

crop fields on which the top 2 or 3 inches of soil has thawed. Under that, the ground is still thoroughly frozen. That mud on top is wet, stays slippery and sticks to everything it touches. It eats 4-wheel-drive pickups for breakfast and lunches on the farm-tractors that come to rescue the trucks!

Getting where you need to go under such conditions means access to heavy-duty, 4x4 ATVs. Usually, you can forget about pulling a trailer, too, so that means lots of trips to bring your decoys and the hunters out

A snow goose up close. Few hunters ever see a snow in this posture!

into the field. If you normally allow 1½ hours to set your spread in a dry or frozen fall field, allow 3 hours to make the same spring set. Bring shovels, winches, come-alongs and pry bars because it's not a case of *if* you'll get stuck, but how often and how far from the road.

Conservation Ethic

While the purpose of the spring season is to reduce the numbers of breeding snow geese, they are still a fine game bird deserving of our respect. Watch the birds that you shoot at until they are out of sight to make sure that one or two don't fall out of the flock. Get after fallen birds immediately. You'll be amazed at how well a wounded white goose can hide itself, even in a plowed field! (Last spring my Lab, Belle, recovered more crippled geese wounded by other hunters than I shot for her myself.)

And, of course, always hunt with a well-trained retriever. They are more ambitious about retrieving the birds over the muddy fields than you or I will ever be. Besides, spring snow goose hunting is a great way to extend your retriever's season. The dog will love you for it!

Finally, be absolutely sure of what you're shooting at. The Canada and white-front geese seem to know that they are protected during the spring season and will seldom hesitate pitching into your decoys. You and your hunting partners should take time to study field-identification closely. Knowing how these birds look and sound will help you avoid mistakes that could cost us these "bonus" days afield. ❖

❖ What Duck Is That? ❖

By Bob Humphrey

The decoys are out. You settle into your blind, check your watch and pour a cup of coffee. Wings whistle in the distance, then the dog perks up his ears and glances skyward. Suddenly, you hear a distinctive rush of air overhead, followed by a pair of gentle splashes. You stand, and two dark shapes vault skyward. Looking down your gun barrel, they seem to dance above the bead momentarily, silhouetted against a pinkish hue. You know they're ducks, but what kind are they? If you don't know, you can't shoot.

In the full light of day, waterfowl identification can sometimes be troublesome, even for experienced hunters. Add the dim lighting conditions that usually accompany the best twilight shooting times, and it can be daunting. And with complicated seasons and limits,

you almost have to be an amateur ornithologist just to stay legal. Still, a little knowledge and experience can go a long way toward helping you decide whether to shoot or pass. The following tips will help you identify waterfowl.

Ducks can be divided into several major groups to aid in identification. Dabblers or puddle ducks are the most common group of freshwater ducks. They are so-called because they feed at or just below the water's surface, sometimes "tipping up" so that only their rear end is exposed.

When swimming, dabblers have a distinct profile that can also help identify them. Relative to their body size, they have long, large wings, which allow them to take off by launching them directly upward off the

Good duck identification skills are critical in the low-light situations so common to waterfowling.

Ducks on the wing, in the fog. What are they?

water's surface. Their landing is also distinctive. They fly in, then flutter down, settling on the water's surface. You can further distinguish teal from the larger dabblers by their smaller size, more rapid wingbeats and erratic flight.

Divers and mergansers, on the other hand, have relatively short wings. In order to take off, they need to build up a head of steam and will skitter along the water's surface for some distance before gaining altitude. The same is true for landing. Rather than dropping in vertically, they typically glide in at a sharp angle, sliding along the water's surface before coming to a halt. Because of the heavier "wing-loading," their wingbeats appear more rapid than that of a puddle duck. They also feed differently, diving beneath the surface and swimming underwater to reach plants, fish and animals that their dabbling cousins cannot. Sea ducks feed, take off and land similarly.

Divers can be further divided into three groups: pochards, bay ducks and mergansers. The pochards—scaups, ring-necked ducks, redheads and canvasbacks—are the group that most resemble the dabblers in profile. Their takeoff and landing, however, is distinctive. Furthermore, the drake's plumage shows a pattern of a dark rump, head and neck with a white or light gray middle. The ring-neck is a smaller, teal-sized bird, and the canvasback's sloping forehead and "delta-shaped" head make it easily distinguishable from the

redhead, which has a rounder head like a dabbler. Bay ducks—buffleheads and goldeneyes—have similar black and white plumage; the hens are duller and grayer. The larger goldeneye sports a white patch between the bill and the eye, while the smaller bufflehead has a large white patch on the back of its head.

Mergansers are almost exclusively fish eaters and have long, narrow, serrated bills. They land and take off in the characteristic diver mode, and even the drab hens show distinct white and dark wing markings in flight. Many hunters shun them because of their fishy flavor. Common mergansers frequent deep rivers and lakes. Hooded mergansers prefer inland freshwater ponds, while red-breasted mergansers occur primarily on coastal marine waters.

Sea ducks can be both easy and hard to identify. Largest and heaviest of the ducks, drake eiders exhibit a distinctive black-and-white pattern and often fly just above the surface of the waves. Hens are a drab brown, but usually stick with their kind. Scoters, on the other hand, can be tough. Both drakes and hens appear as a nearly uniform dark color. Their only distinguishing characteristics are a few subtle white markings on the wings of drakes. Surf scoters, sometimes called skunkheads, have white patches on the front and back of their head. The white-winged scoter gets its name from small white patches on its wings, which are conspicuous only in flight. The aptly named black scoter is sooty colored, except for an orange knob on the base of its bill.

Last of the group, the oldsquaw, is the teal of the sea. Its much smaller size, sometimes erratic flight and black-and-white markings make it difficult to confuse with other sea ducks.

Habitat and location can also help you trim the list of potential candidates considerably, through process of elimination. If you're hunting anywhere along the Atlantic Flyway, for instance, your chances of seeing a cinnamon teal are slim, and if you're gunning over an inland beaver pond, you can probably rule out sea ducks. In general, when hunting over shallow, freshwater marshes and ponds, you're most likely to encounter dabblers or puddle ducks like mallards, black ducks, pintails, wigeon and teal. On deeper freshwater, you might have a few dabblers, but you're more likely to see divers. On coastal waters, you're hunting primarily sea ducks.

These are generalizations, however, and exceptions always occur. On freshwater marshes bordering larger, deeper water, you might encounter ring-necked ducks and hooded mergansers. You could encounter green-winged teal and black ducks anywhere from shallow puddles to coastal salt marshes and estuaries. While they prefer deeper water, buffleheads can also be found feeding in the creeks of coastal marshes. Mallards will occasionally buzz a spread of diver decoys on big water, and red-breasted mergansers and goldeneyes are a common sight when gunning sea ducks on the ocean.

Because of the difficulty in identifying waterfowl, many states use a point system rather than a species-specific bag limit. This allows hunters to shoot first and ask questions later. With a little practice or a field guide, drakes can be easily identified in the hand. But even to the trained eye, hens can sometimes pose a problem. Also, early season hunters might sometimes encounter drakes that are still in their summer or "eclipse" plumage, which closely resembles that of the hen's. This is especially true for teal. This is an adaptation to the brief, flightless period when ducks molt their flight feathers, and the drab mottled plumage usually associated with hens helps camouflage them from predators.

All ducks can be identified by their wings. The primary characteristic to look for is the speculum, which is a patch of color on the secondary wing feathers of all ducks. The mallard's speculum is iridescent blue, with white stripes above and below. The black duck's is similarly colored, but lacks one or both white stripes. The pintail has a green speculum, like that of the green-winged teal. The gadwall is the only puddle duck that shows a white speculum in flight, while the wigeon has a green speculum with white shoulders. The shoveler, blue-winged teal and cinnamon teal have green speculums with powder-blue shoulders. The shoveler is larger and has a distinctive spoon-shaped bill.

One more group not previously mentioned are tree ducks. The wood duck is common in freshwater marshes along the Atlantic and Mississippi flyways. It's also one of our most spectacular ducks, and its col-

In the timber, snap duck identification is necessary, or the shot opportunity will be gone.

oration and crested head make it easily identifiable. Its flight is often erratic, like the teal's, and the birds are vocal, often emitting a high-pitched whining whistle in flight. The range of the black-bellied and fulvous whistling duck is limited largely to the Gulf Coast and southern Florida, and they prefer wooded wetlands. The black belly and pink bill of the former make it easily distinguishable from the fulvous. The ruddy duck is the only North American representative of a tribe referred to as the stiff-tailed ducks. It's a small, stocky bird with a broad, flat bill and prefers marshy areas along lake and pond margins.

Dedicated waterfowlers should consider carrying a field guide and good binoculars. Binoculars can help you identify ducks at a distance and are a great way to pass time between flights. Any good field guide to birds will have a section on waterfowl. Many show the birds at rest and in flight. The U.S. Fish and Wildlife Service publishes a pocket-sized booklet titled, "Ducks at a Distance: A Waterfowl Identification Guide," which is usually available free at refuges and other federal facilities. Another good book is *The Sibley Guide to Birds*. It has color drawings, range maps and vocalizations. This book is widely available in bookstores and contains more than 30 pages of waterfowl identification aides. ❖

A Duck Identification Quiz

A

These are extremely graceful and fast flyers, fond of zig-zagging from great heights before leveling off to land. Their longs necks and tails make them appear to be much larger than they actually are.

B

The most common of the dabblers, this duck is found in all flyways. Distinguishing characteristics include a metallic green head and bright blue speculums with white bars along both leading and trailing edges.

C

This small, compact diving duck is often seen in large flocks as it makes its way south for the winter. Its distinctive black-and-white plumage and blue bill aid in identification, but watch out for look-alikes.

D

Normally late to start south, these ducks migrate in line and irregular "V"s. Their wing-beat is rapid and noisy. They have a long, sloping forehead and peaked crown that produce a distinctive profile.

E

These large dabblers are nervous and quick to alarm. Their flight is fast, irregular, with many twists and turns. In a bunched flock, their movements have been compared to those of pigeons.

F

Their small size and twisting-and-turning flight give the illusion of great speed. Small, compact flocks fly low over marshes and often take hunters by surprise. High-pitched peeping is common.

ANSWERS: (A) *Northern Pintail* (B) *Mallard* (C) *Lesser Scaup (bluebill)* (D) *Canvasback* (E) *American Wigeon* (F) *Blue-Winged Teal*

RANK: (5–6) *Dr. Duck* (3–4) *Almost Ducky* (1–2) *Back to Duck School* (0) *Need a Seeing-eye Lab*

❖ Belated Bobwhites ❖

By Bryan Hendricks

After hours of trudging across sandhills and busting through brush in the Texas Panhandle, Danny Pierce and I had but two quail to show for our trouble. For the moment, however, they were all that we needed to provide a few good photographs.

As Pierce proudly hoisted his quail in a variety of poses, I rolled, slithered and crawled through sand, burrs and weeds trying to get the perfect angle. Meanwhile, his dogs sniffed the area like vacuum cleaners as I locked my knees in the middle of a clump of bluestem. Satisfied with my work, I stood and brushed myself off amid a cloud of dust and sand that erupted from my clothes in the wind.

My heart lodged in my throat when, from between my legs, a quail burst from the clump of bluestem. We watched in astonishment as it fluttered up and sailed into a distant thicket.

One gorgeous game bird.

In a nutshell, that's the essence of late-season quail hunting. Birds hold tight in the smallest pieces of cover, and you can lie on top of them without knowing it.

"Late-season quail hunting presents different challenges that can change from one week to the next, and sometimes from day to day," said Steve DeMaso, upland game supervisor for the Texas Parks and Wildlife Department. "The upside is that your dogs are probably going to be at their peak performance if you've been working them steadily. If you hunt a lot, you're probably going to be in better physical condition than you were earlier in the season, which will allow you to cover more ground."

Hunters who get spoiled on the covey rises of November and December often have a hard time hunting in the waning days of the season. The birds have been pointed, chased and shot at so often that the survivors are extremely skittish.

Late in the season, quail tend to wander alone or in pairs, especially during the middle of the day, and if a hard-charging pointer gets on their trail in open country, they're going to run. That's why you see so many false points in late December and January. Hunting conditions depend largely on the weather, but in the heart of Midwestern quail country, including Oklahoma, Texas, Kansas and Nebraska, you never know what the weather will hold. The past two winters were mild and dry, but a standard winter on the plains is cold, windy and snowy.

Warm, dry weather usually produces poor scenting conditions, which make it difficult for dogs to find birds. Cold, moist weather with a light breeze is ideal. Moist air helps concentrate bird scent, while dry air disperses it.

Early in the day, the best places to find quail are near grassy creekbottoms with brushy cover nearby. Coveys frequently remain intact until late morning, and you can often get a good covey rise near small- to medium-sized brush thickets.

In the late season, know quails' daily habits to decide where to hunt at what time of day.

In the middle of the day, quail loaf in dusty areas with a protective overhead canopy, such as plum thickets or woodlots.

By late afternoon, they move into the open to feed, and you can often find them foraging on grassy hillsides until just before sundown.

During a three-day hunt with DeMaso and Pierce last January near Wheeler, Texas, we followed that pattern for some memorable hunting. Almost daily, we got at least one good covey rise in a creekbottom and another around noon in a plum thicket. We spent the rest of the day chasing singles and doubles, but they were plentiful enough to keep us alert.

In the final hours of the last day, we hit paydirt. The sun was starting to melt over the horizon when we turned the dogs loose on a large, rolling pasture of big bluestem. The first two hills produced nothing, but one hill dipped a little deeper than the rest. As we climbed the other side, Pierce's dogs went on point in different places. Across the hill, DeMaso's pointer, Angie, was also locked down.

"There are birds all over this hillside!" DeMaso shouted. "Make sure that you stay close to the dogs!"

Pierce immediately folded a single, but another bird was sitting tight in a clump of bluestem. I approached the dog from the left quarter until I stood over the grass clump. The dog, still on point, quivered like the E-string on a bass guitar.

For years, quail populations have been declining across the nation. In the Southeast, for example, quail are pretty much a thing of the past. The story is the same in states like Oklahoma, which has long prided itself as one of the top five quail hunting destinations. Quail are disappearing because their habitat is disappearing.

Steve DeMaso, upland game supervisor for the Texas Parks and Wildlife Department, says that in many cases the habitat changes so slowly and gradually that it's hardly noticeable. Compare an old photograph of an area with a recent one, however, and the changes are obvious. Poorly maintained grasslands are growing into thick forests or are being converted into vast grain fields with no edge habitat for quail. Elsewhere, good quail habitat is being replaced with housing developments, parking lots and shopping centers.

Fortunately, it's not too late, because quail have friends in high places. Harland Stonecipher, chairman of the Oklahoma Wildlife Conservation Commission, recently declared that restoring quail habitat would be a priority for the Oklahoma Department of Wildlife Conservation during his term. The key to restoring quail populations, he says, is to work more closely with private landowners to identify needs and provide them with technical assistance.

One of the most interesting projects is taking place in Arkansas, but it has nothing to do with quail. In the Poteau and Mena districts of the Ouachita National Forest, the U.S. Forest Service (USFS) converted nearly 200,000 acres of forest in western Arkansas to provide habitat for the endangered red-cockaded woodpecker. Through a regimen of selective timber harvest and prescribed fire, the USFS removed the thick understory that once dominated the area, allowing native grasses to reclaim the forest floor. An unexpected benefit has been an explosion of bobwhite quail. They're so abundant that Warren Montague, the USFS district biologist who manages the project, has dubbed an unnamed logging road in the area "Seven Covey Road."

The recipe is simple. To have quail, you must have quail habitat. Since most of America's quail habitat is privately owned, landowners will determine the future of the bobwhite quail.

I kicked the grass with my right foot. Nothing.
I kicked it again, harder.
I swear that I could feel the wind from its wingbeats as a bobwhite thundered up past my chin. He bobbed and weaved across the hillside, but I dropped him with one shot. We had about 30 minutes of sensational shooting, all on singles and doubles, which lasted until the sky turned orange.

In late January of the previous year, I enjoyed an equally productive hunt in a different environment. I was hunting with a couple of U.S. Forest Service (USFS) biologists in the piney woods of Ouachita National Forest in western Arkansas. Near the end of the hunt, a sore knee slowed me down and separated me from my companions. I followed a narrow draw up a hill into some thick timber when I chanced upon a battered, old pointer owned by USFS technician Ray Yelverton. The dog was locked down on a solid point in front of a small brush thicket.

Easing into position, I shouldered my shotgun and barked, "Get 'em up, boy!"

The dog lurched forward, and a covey of about 30 birds spurted up and away like a sack full of Roman candles. I rolled a pair with three shots from my slide-action 12 gauge.

It was a typical late-season hunt. The birds were wary and tenacious, and they brought out the best in a fine hunting dog. ❖

❖ Frosty Pheasants ❖

By Mark Kayser

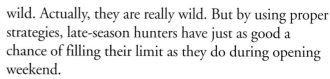

Why is it that everyone thinks that they have to be out hunting on opening morning? It doesn't matter if it's for doves or elk, hunters can't bear to miss the first day of the season. I'm no different. I guess that it's the anticipation of waiting all year to go afield. When it comes to pheasants, opening weekend for me is more about socializing with friends, gorging on food and watching young pups go squirrelly chasing ringnecks.

But it's toward the end of the season when I get serious about hunting birds. By then, most other seasons are winding down, leaving me more time to focus on pheasants. Most bird hunters have had their fill of chasing ringnecks and switch hats and take on the role of armchair quarterback. Add to this the fact that public land is vacant and landowners are often more approachable, warmed by holiday spirits and fewer hunters kicking up dust down their driveways.

With all these positives, why wouldn't you wait until the late season? Okay, the birds might be a bit more

wild. Actually, they are really wild. But by using proper strategies, late-season hunters have just as good a chance of filling their limit as they do during opening weekend.

My good friend, outdoor writer and native South Dakotan, Ron Spomer, probably had more to do with switching me to late-season hunting than anything, or anyone. Spomer religiously returns to South Dakota over the holiday season and pleads with me to line up some pre-holiday pheasant hunting, regardless of the wintry conditions. Whether we pursue birds in shelterbelts or Conservation Reserve Program (CRP) acres, we generally find success.

Before heading afield late in the season, it pays to know a little about pheasants and their lifestyle after the first frost. On opening weekend, hunters have the advantage of pursuing young-of-the-year birds, but by midseason most of those birds are stiff in a freezer.

Pheasants in December choose different hideouts than they did in October. Instead of agricultural fields and fencelines, roosters move to cattail sloughs, wooded draws and mature farmsteads or adjoining shelterbelts.

Cover needs to be large enough to catch snow on its north and west sides, yet allow plenty of cover free of snow on its south and east sides.

How soon pheasants begin utilizing this cover and how many use it depend on the arrival of Old Man Winter and its severity. The past three winters in the pheasant belt of the upper Midwest have been mild, and pheasants have remained dispersed instead of crowded into the tighter quarters of winter habitat. But take a winter like the upper Midwest experienced during 1996–97, and without quality habitat, winter mortality would have soared well above the 50 percent range that many areas reported.

Today, the Great Plains harbors the highest pheasant populations, beginning in Kansas and working north through the Dakotas. Since pheasants crowd into the limited winter habitat found in this region, getting close to a group of wintering birds is about as difficult as getting close to a herd of pronghorns in a sage basin. The multitude of eyes in the crowded cover allows for quick danger detection.

So now you know where to look for late-season birds and that they'll most likely be bunched in large flocks. But how does one go about getting close to them? For solo hunters or small party hunting groups, it pays to scout small, extremely thick patches of cover. Targeting small areas allows you to hunt more thoroughly with less chance of birds escaping. The goal of hunting smaller pockets is to pressure the roosters into remaining hidden and not flushing. That's where a good flushing dog or retriever earns its Alpo. Pressured roosters dig down deep into cattails and burrow under cedars and plum bushes. Without a dog, odds are good that you'll walk by a tight-sitting rooster.

If you don't have a dog, a couple of fast-moving hunters can still find success in the late season by moving quickly through cover, stopping periodically to flush nerve-wracked birds. This tactic works well in CRP acres and small pockets of cover alike. But when attacking any late-season hotspot, approach it quietly. Then move quickly through the cover, zigzagging back and forth, pushing the birds to an open area where they'll feel insecure. Of course, the bulk of the birds will flush wildly out of shotgun range, but a few birds surprised by the quick attack will hold tight and won't flush until you nearly step on them. And as you stop periodically and quietly wait, many will flush from the tension.

Look for late-season pheasants in extremely heavy cover like wooded draws, shelterbelts and cattail swamps.

One of my favorite late-season methods is to sneak in and wait for pheasants to fly into roosting cover. Once I see a rooster land, I pinpoint the spot and hustle over to try and flush the bird before he moves or the sun sets. This works great in less densely populated areas where birds don't inundate a roosting locale. Again, moving quickly for the element of surprise is key. Remember, when moving quickly with a firearm, keep it pointed in a safe direction and keep the action open, closing it before surprising the bird.

If you hunt in large groups, the late season can also offer great hunting. But don't approach a field like you did in October. Again, a stealthy, quiet approach needs to be the plan. Before the walkers even approach the area, the blockers should sneak quietly into position. Besides being quiet, they should also be inconspicuous on the horizon, but not to the point of being out of sight to the walkers. Instead of hunkering down in the weeds, slide up tight to a fence post or tree, and wear plenty of orange to alert others of your presence.

If the walkers want to have any chance for a shot, they need to park well out of sight; don't slam car doors, and use cat-like moves to get into position. Once in the field, zigzagging is also necessary to flush tight-sitting cocks, but with walkers at the other end, there is no need to speed through the field.

Late-season hunting can be just as productive as hunting in the early season, but instead of joking around the pickup truck, hunters need to take a whitetail-like look at their pheasant hunting strategy.

If you start the hunt quietly, you'll have plenty of opportunities at the end of the hunt for back-slapping and socializing with a brace of late-season roosters in hand. ❖

❖ CHRISTMAS GROUSE ❖

By Gordy Krahn

It was Christmas day and my younger brother, Tony, and I were walking side-by-side down a snow-covered logging trail that meandered through a tangled spruce and cedar swamp. We were carrying on a tradition that stretches back more than 25 years. After a hearty holiday meal at my folks' house, we had gathered our hunting gear and headed for Minnesota's Beltrami Island State Forest just south of town. Grouse were near the peak of their 10-year population cycle, and hunting early in the season had been fabulous.

Tattoo, my young Brittany, got a nose full of bird before we had walked 100 yards down the dim road,

Late-season grouse hunting is not about filling bag limits, but spending an enjoyable wintry day in the woods with your best buddy.

flash pointing and then frantically circling a cluster of tall, bushy spruce, nose plowing through the fresh snow.

"It's gotta be up in one of these trees," Tony said as we circled the base of each spruce methodically, looking up, trying to discern grouse from growth. The bird held tight for a full five minutes, and we probably would have given up if Tattoo had not insisted that there was a bird close by. Finally, the bird bolted and Tony dropped it with a single shot from his 12 gauge. I slapped him on the back as Tattoo dropped the bird at our feet. Every December grouse is a trophy well earned.

Tony missed another bird later that day and I never fired a shot during the three hours that we were in the woods. Not a great day if we were concerned with such things as filling our bag limits. We weren't. We had long since realized that late-season grouse hunting isn't about numbers. It's about spending an enjoyable day in the frosty woods, and the challenge of matching wits with the birds.

Hunting ruffed grouse late in the season is a sport for only the most passionate birders. Grouse are nervous and flighty and hang out in the meanest cover that they can find. Forget about those honey holes where you found coveys of young birds early in the season. Winter grouse gravitate to thick cover along the edges of grassy swamps where two-legged and four-legged predators hesitate to venture. Forget, too, the calm indifference that they displayed early in the season. Those birds are in the freezer or have become highly educated by the time December rolls around.

One constant is that ruffed grouse, early or late, are sprinters. Hampered by short wings and a small heart, they rarely fly more than 60 yards, and the resolute hunter, with or without a pooch, can often get multiple flushes from a single bird. When I put a bird to wing and don't make the shot, I try to determine the direction of its flight, which is typically straight away from danger. At the predictable 50- or 60-yard mark, the birds invariably hook right or left just before landing.

I typically work the thick cover of transition zones that divide the edges of grassy swamps and spruce, cedar or jack pine woods. Birds love this stuff late in the season. They generally hang close to the edges of this cover so that they can exercise the option of flight if they are discovered.

My dog gets the brush-busting duty. I send him 20 or 30 yards into the heavy cover and walk the edges, hoping that he will flush a bird in my direction. Being a pointer of a somewhat steady nature, he will hold on birds that hunker down and hide. But he will most likely bust any nervous birds to flight. When Tony and I hunt together, we generally walk about 30 yards apart and let the dog work between us.

Another favorite tactic involves patrolling the back roads after a fresh snow. Grouse often meander around early in the morning in search of food and their tell-tale tracks can lead to feathered treasure. Grouse, by nature, are walkers. They only take to flight to escape danger or to fly up into trees where they feed on aspen and birch buds. I have walked down many grouse by following their tracks immediately following a snow shower.

Late-season grouse hunting is not an activity for casual hunters, or those who measure success by the heft of their game pouches. Rather, it's a sport for outdoorsmen who cannot bear to stay indoors on a crisp winter morning. Forget about numbers and instead relish a heart-warming, toe-numbing walk into a winter wonderland of late-season grouse. ❖

❖ HUNTING THE MIXED BAG ❖

By Gordy Krahn

For a split second, I knew precisely what it feels like to be a mouse. The desert bobcat was closing the precious little ground between us at an alarming rate, its eye (the second was milky white) focused on the slight movement of my hand working the end of the closed-reed cottontail tube. She wasn't getting the big picture.

I panned the gun to meet the cat's advance just as Larry O. Gates let out a lip-squeak that brought the feline to an abrupt halt just 18 steps away. The Model 788 barked as the 55-grainer left the barrel catbound. A millisecond later, the bobette was rugged out on the high-desert duff. I was hunting on the San Carlos Apache Indian Reservation east of Phoenix, Arizona, with friends, Gerry Blair, Larry O. Gates and Gary "The Slammer" Hull. That expanse covers nearly 2 million acres of pure biodiversity. Forests of plush ponderosa pine, alligator juniper, oak and pinyon pine—high desert dissected by brush-choked canyons and obtrusive rimrock. Predator heaven.

Larry and I had hiked in and set up just after high noon on the rim of a deep, brushy ravine that overlooked a creek-bed far below. We were backed up against the sparse cover offered by a few scattered yuccas. It was the kind of setup that could produce any of the predators that call the San Carlos home. And while I had expected that the stand might summon a coyote or two, even with the sun at its peak—and set up for such—I was delighted and surprised to see the cat working the day shift. By the end of our three-day outing, we

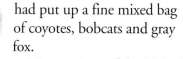

had put up a fine mixed bag of coyotes, bobcats and gray fox.

Most regions of the United States have two or more major predatory species utilizing the same habitat, competing for a community food source. In parts of the East, red and gray fox ranges overlap and are intertwined with those of the coyote, bobcat and raccoon. Out West, coyotes, gray fox, bobcats and mountain lions commonly shop the same friendly neighborhood grocery store for mammalian, feathered or crawly delectables.

This provides a delightful dilemma for the equal-opportunity predator hunter. Consequently, every time a hunter cuts loose on his favorite predator call, he has no way of knowing what might show up for dinner. The best way to deal with this situation is to expect the unexpected and plan for the unplanned.

Gerry, an Arizona hunter with nearly 50 years of predator hunting experience, and I had time to deliberate this topic while on the San Carlos. We hunted an entire day after a major storm without raising so much as a flea. That gave us plenty of time for discussion.

"Much of the time, a hunter sights in on a target species as he or she selects the calling country and the calling stand within that country," Gerry said in regard to hunting the mixed bag. "Even so, here in the West and in much of the East, an uncalled customer might respond. Western hunters who target coyotes in a greasewood flat, as an example, might draw a bobcat or gray fox from the mesquite-lined wash to his back. I take the time needed to evaluate the land and the response potential at each setup. Doing so causes me to perceive sneakers that might otherwise stay discreet."

The Predator Equation

If you recollect anything from 8th-grade math (I had to look these up) you might remember terminology such as "common denominator" and "variables." By Webster's definition, common denominator refers to "... a number that can be evenly divided by all of the denominators of a set of fractions." In simpler terms, it refers to those things that have something in common. Variables are those things that are inconsistent or different from other things.

By now you're probably wondering what the heck this has to do with predator hunting. Actually, these concepts apply to hunting the mixed bag and illustrate the importance of analyzing each hunting situation for optimum results. Let me explain.

First, ask yourself what commonalties are shared by the predator species that inhabit the areas where you hunt. Write these down. Come on, humor me.

First and foremost, predators are naturally going to share a common food source, such as rabbits, rodents, birds—maybe even deer or pronghorns. And don't forget plant matter and domestic fare. This can affect how they utilize their environment while on the prowl for food.

In addition to knowing what animals eat, Gerry says that knowing their habits and how they use their habitat to obtain that food can provide a deadly advantage to hunters.

"Knowing that a bobcat is often a sneak," he said, "one that prefers the safety of cover, can provide an insight into its approach. Those new to the sport (even some not-so-new) become so focused on calling and killing a red fox, for instance, that they do not evaluate the land around the stand. Their setup might be effective against the red that they expect to respond, but less effective against the coyote, bobcat or raccoon that might make a surprise visit."

What other similarities come to mind? Predators typically utilize the same water sources, the same cover, the same travel routes and so on. You get the picture. These are examples of the things that the predators in your

area hold in common. It is the reason they live there and it's how they survive.

Variables

Next, let's look at the variables. Animal hunting techniques might vary. Some predators work the night shift while others hunt during daylight hours. Coyotes prefer open spaces in the West, while cats and gray fox are more likely to work heavy cover. In the East, it is common for coyotes to frequent big timber, while red fox hunt open farm fields and pastures.

And how do they hunt? A feline, being a creeper, might take a half-hour or more to make its way to call, while coyotes and gray fox, often chargers, are more likely to show within the first few minutes of a stand.

Then there's the difference in how they use their sensory systems. Felines, for example, are visual hunters, using their keen eyesight to detect and stalk their prey, while canines depend primarily upon their olfactory senses.

Now that you've analyzed the commonalties and differences between the predators that you hunt, how can we apply this knowledge to hunting situations?

Take a look at the list that you've just compiled, and an equation should emerge that will allow you to take better advantage of hunting a multi-species area. Let's apply this information to the equipment you use, stand selection and calling techniques to get you started.

Bobcats are sneakers by nature and often take their time when responding to the call. Plan on spending at least 30 minutes if your setup is in good cat country.

Gun Selection

Using the common denominator/variables equation, you will quickly note that no single gun is going to be the right choice under all conditions. A caliber that will rug out a 130-pound desert lion, say .22-250 Rem. on up, will kill a 10-pound gray fox occupying the same territory a whole lot deader than need be. And that same long-range rifle topped with a high-power scope will not serve you well in the brushy cover of the East or the desert tangles or woody canyons of the West. Some compromise must be made in regard to sure-kill potential and fur recovery as well as long- vs. short-range shot opportunities.

Let's look at some of the fur guns that would apply to the predators that you might encounter, and let's see if we can spot any common denominators.

In the West, opportunity for long shots exist. And your choice of firearms should reflect that possibility. Calibers such as .22-250 Rem., .25-06 Rem. and .243 Win. immediately come to mind. These and other like calibers will reach out and touch predators at a considerable distance and can handle the largest Western canines and felines. But you might sacrifice some fur as you step up muscle to obtain long-range accuracy.

Like most Western callers, Gerry packs two guns, a rifle and a shotgun, in the pickup truck and lets the stand dictate which stays behind. "I call pretty much the same for the big three: coyotes, fox and bobcats," he said. "If I am teamed up, I might carry a shotgun in close country, asking that my partner carry a rifle, or vice versa. When solo calling, I almost always carry a rifle of a caliber that's stout enough to whack the bashful bobcat or the cougar that might hang up a couple of football fields away."

In the East, where human occupancy and tight terrain is common, long-range shooting opportunities are somewhat diminished, and the above-mentioned calibers often supply more horsepower than is necessary, especially in fox country. Eastern hunters might consider some of the "Mighty Mouse" calibers such as the .17 Rem., .22 Hornet, .222 Rem. or .223 Rem. Keep in mind, however, that the Eastern coyote is a large and sturdy animal which might require more killing than a 10-pound fox. If you are hunting in proven coyote country, your gun choice should provide the foot-pounds of energy needed to topple a 40-pound-plus coyote.

A rule of thumb is to use a caliber that will be hefty enough for the largest predator that you might encounter, but will keep fur damage minimal on the smallest. Of course, there is no such animal, so the best that you can hope for is choosing a caliber and gun setup that falls somewhere in the middle. As a guideline, the .22-250 Rem. is considered a good fur gun in the West, and the .223 Rem. serves as a good Eastern fur-getter.

And don't discount the value of a shotgun in tight country, or when working the night shift. In heavy cover, where action is likely to be fast and fierce, a scattergun loaded with buckshot or BBs is often your best choice. This is a lethal fur-taker at close range, and pelt damage is typically minimal. Many Eastern hunters prefer to use shotguns at night for safety considerations.

Stand Selection

When hunting areas where two or more predatory species might be present, take time to analyze your stand selection. On the San Carlos, the terrain transcended from open range to brush-choked canyons to obtrusive rimrock. And animal sign was a constant reminder that lions, bobcats, gray fox and coyotes were all using the landscape with varying degrees of regularity. We found that setting up on large open expanses usually gave up coyotes, and the brushy canyons and rimrock were where the lions, bobcats and gray fox hung out.

When I hunt the East, I typically set up in transition zones from heavy cover to some type of opening. Most critters like to hug the heavy cover before committing to calls and breaking out into the open.

Know what each animal prefers in respect to home range and its hunting technique and then set up accordingly. In areas where cats are as likely as canines to come to the call, you must prepare for critters working the wind as well as those scanning the landscape for movement.

If the lay of the land allows, it is best to set up with the wind in your face overlooking the areas from which you expect your company to arrive. But you must also account for the fact that some animals are going to try to get in behind you. Use a natural barrier such as a water source or some other obstruction to prevent them from circling your position.

Set up similarly in a crosswind. If the animal approaches downwind in your shooting lane, it will not pick up on your scent until it's too late. If the wind is blowing from right to left, I like to keep an open shooting lane to my left to detect any animal that might be circling downwind. I find that setting up in a crosswind works well when the wind is blowing at a pretty good clip.

If I'm hunting a wide-open area with good visibility, I sometimes set up about two-thirds up a hill and call downwind. The predators will generally work from one side or the other to the downwind position trying to pick up my scent. A high-powered rifle on a steady rest will usually pick these up before they detect you.

Calling Techniques

You've no doubt heard that canines come more quickly to the call than do cats. And the majority of the time, this is true. But not all predators subscribe to these, or any set of rules. My San Carlos cat, for example, appeared only 10 minutes into the scream and at high noon, to boot. The reason ... who knows?

Most Western callers rarely spend more than 15 to 20 minutes at a stand where coyotes are expected and rarely exceed 30 to 40 minutes when bobcats and lions are the called critters. Eastern callers, because of the heavier cover and tighter terrain, should extend those parameters a bit. In fact, I know a successful caller in Vermont who sits on each stand no less than 45 minutes and has customers sneak in well past the time when most hunters would have packed it in. If heavy cover is typical where you hunt, you can expect predators to use that cover to put the sneak on your position, so remain alert at all times.

Whether you're hunting the expansive West, the woodlands of the East or the prairie grasslands, knowing your quarry well and how each uses its terrain will help you solve the predator hunting puzzle. And take a tip from your 8th-grade math teacher: Use common denominators and variables to take the best advantage of the opportunities of the mixed bag, because you never know what might show up for dinner. ❖

Combination guns, such as this Crossfire LLC, provide a double-dose of trouble for predators.

Double Trouble

When hunting buddy-style, it is often a good idea for one hunter to carry a rifle, while the other brings a scatter-gun to the stand. Should a paranoid customer hang up in the open, out of shotgun range, the rifleman can do the dirty work. The shotgun will provide an advantage when animals show up quickly without warning.

Some solo hunters carry two guns to the stand. They typically hold the shotgun at the ready for the hard-chargers, but have a flat-shooting rifle handy for those critters that give them the bad-eye a couple of football fields away.

Two gun manufactures have put another option in the hands of predator hunters. Crossfire LLC offers a slide-action gun that chambers four 12 gauge shotshells and five .223 rifle rounds in one gun. The gun can be switched from rifle to scattergun with the flick of a switch.

Savage Arms Inc. offers the break-open Model 24F Combination Gun, which chambers a single 12 gauge shell and either a .223 Rem. or .22 Hornet for predator work.

If you've ever lugged a shotgun and rifle together through the forest or across the prairie, you'll really appreciate these combination guns. You're able to take the young coyote that charges in like he hasn't had a meal for weeks ... or nail that sneaky red fox that hangs way out there with a suspicious look.

HUNTING COYOTES WITH MAN'S BEST FRIEND

By Mark Kayser

If you enjoy hunting coyotes, I bet you'll never look at your family pooch the same way again after reading this article. A new but slowly growing technique is making its way into the public arena. For at least two decades, a number of animal damage control (ADC) agents have been using dogs to hunt coyotes, and their years of trial-and-error efforts confirm one thing: Using dogs increases hunter success.

No, these professionals are not chasing coyotes with dogs, like hunters do for mountain lions or bears. Rather, it would be better described as a game of "catch me if you can." The dog actually provokes the coyote and lures it back to the waiting hunter. Sound exciting? I've witnessed it, and even though I live in the middle of the best upland hunting in the world, my next pooch purchase is not going to be bred for birds. Rather, it's going to be a Wile E. Coyote hunting dog.

What makes dogs want to hunt coyotes, and why

would a coyote chase a dog? These questions date back 35 million years, when the first canines began appearing in fossil records. At that time, there was little differentiation between canine species. That changed about 10 million years ago. Canines began taking on characteristics of present-day dogs and coyotes, and they quickly populated the world. Still, it wasn't until 50,000 years ago that wild canines were domesticated by humans to become the family pets that we cherish today.

Simply put, coyotes are dogs, and dogs are coyotes. They are cousins, and like all mammals—including humans—instinctively protect territory, food and family.

A natural rivalry exists between closely related species like coyotes and dogs. If something intrudes upon their space, they defend it. A domestic dog intruding into a coyote's territory is no different than a stranger walking into your living room. You would make a stand, just as a coyote will against a dog.

I'd heard many tales from ADC agents in South Dakota about the effectiveness of using dogs to lure or "decoy" coyotes into range. But witnessing it firsthand blew my mind. My brother-in-law, Jerry Murphy, wanted to show me how his black Labrador retriever, Dixie, decoyed coyotes. Being a native South Dakotan, I know that black Labs have two roles in life: retrieving downed birds and keeping the carpet warm adjacent to their masters' recliners.

Our first morning calling session brought nothing into range, but our second stand produced a quick response. Only one problem arose: The coyote wouldn't approach to investigate the dog. Frustrated, Murphy moved closer to the coyote. For a few brief seconds, he was in full view of the coyote. The coyote watched intently, but didn't leave its post on the gumbo knob.

Using a ridge to hide his and Dixie's approach, Murphy moved to within 400 yards of the coyote, while I watched nearly 1,000 yards in the distance. As Murphy climbed a ridge for a better look, Dixie bolted over the top and caught the attention of the coyote. The coyote paced back and forth, then shot from the top of the hill in pursuit of the dog. Sensing danger, Dixie swung back toward Murphy.

Murphy didn't realize that the race had begun and

appeared from behind the ridge, showing himself to the approaching coyote. The coyote quickly applied the brakes and retreated back into the gumbo gullies. If Murphy hadn't made the untimely appearance, it would have ended up within easy shotgun range.

For a coyote hunting addict like me, the show was enough to get me shopping for coyote hunting dogs.

The reward of a successful coyote hunt.

So will the family dachshund work? Probably not, but most breeds of dogs with some lung and leg behind them have a chance. Merv Griswold, a six-year veteran of coyote decoying, has used everything from a German short-haired pointer to an Airedale crossed with a Jack Russell terrier. What does this Gillette, Wyoming, hunting guide recommend?

"I'm partial to mountain curs. They are as close to a recipe-type coyote dog as you can get," Griswold said. "Chris McAllister, an ADC agent in South Dakota, has been researching mountain curs and from his field work, believes that they are the perfect breed, combining an instinctive nature to hunt and enough stamina to harass the coyotes into the chase. My cur is a 3-year-old and she is working great."

Whether you decide to use your Labrador retriever or purchase a mountain cur, be aware that it takes hours of coyote interaction for a dog to understand the concept of provoking a coyote into chasing it back to within shooting range.

Most ADC experts put their dogs into coyote situations during the spring when depredation increases with young livestock on the ground. Coyotes adamantly defend their den sites and will chase off any intruders. I've even had a female coyote chase my horse, with me on it, while protecting her den site.

Different Strokes

Another point that the experts make is that not all dogs react the same to hunting coyotes. Some dogs, regardless of breed, do not have an instinctive drive to pursue their cousins. Others might have the drive, but they go about it in a different manner.

"The dogs that I like to work with actually go out and hunt the coyote, then bring it back to my shooting location," Griswold said. "Some dogs, though, like to sit next to their master until a coyote is spotted, then run out to harass it back to the shooter's location."

One of my friends uses his dog as a decoy, making it sit in a location away from him until a coyote responds to his call. Then he calls to the dog to come, and the coyotes tend to follow into shooting range.

Even though the experts agree that decoying coyotes with a dog works best in the spring, they also agree that it can increase hunting success in the fall and winter.

And based on a coyote's territorial instincts, it should work across North America with some fine-tuning for your neck of the woods.

Although coyote expert Mark Miller has not used this technique in his home state of Indiana, he sees no reason why it wouldn't work in Eastern states.

"I'm certain that decoying coyotes with dogs would work. Coyotes are coyotes, East or West. They have a definite territory and are protective of it. Using dogs threatens that territory and causes a confrontation," Miller says.

The key to making this technique work for any area is tailoring it to the territory. Miller points out that in the East, coyotes have a smaller, more defined territory and their populations are more dense. They also tend to move less than their Western cousins do during daylight hours.

Hunters need to locate these territories and try to evaluate bedding areas to move in close for an initial confrontation, or as Miller says, "... get right in and mix it up with them." Another reason to pressure coyotes into a confrontation is the fact that Eastern coyotes regularly see and hear dogs because there are more farms and hobby acreage per square mile. Pressuring coyotes by entering their bedrooms should get their attention, though.

Setting Up

Tactics for decoying coyotes resemble typical winter coyote calling setups, except for one detail: You have a dog running amuck in front of you. Hunters need good visibility. Sit high on a ridge, or in a haystack with plenty of open ground in front of your calling location. Calling in thick stands of trees or brush allows a coyote to circle undetected and does not allow the dog a good view to spot approaching coyotes.

Most hunters prefer to have the wind in their face, causing the coyote to come in and circle. Remarkably, many coyotes, while chasing dogs, throw all caution to the wind and ignore human scent, even after getting a snout full.

Begin a setup by using territorial howls, then wait at least five minutes. The dog can be out hunting, running or merely loafing. Many times, a coyote will approach the howling site to investigate an intruder. If a coyote

Using a dog, even the family Lab, can be an effective means of decoying coyotes sure-kill close.

doesn't appear, go into a series of prey-in-distress calls such as rabbits, deer or even another canine. If nothing appears after 15 minutes, try another round of howls, and then move to fresh ground if nothing shows.

Coyotes have little protection in most states, but be sure to check game regulations before experimenting with this tactic. Some states regulate using dogs in pursuing game, and others have rules pertaining to live decoys.

Although no hunting technique assures 100 percent success, when this tactic works, 100 percent excitement is the result. Besides, it's a great substitute for walking the dog. ❖ **Editor's Note:** *Check regulations to assure that using dogs to hunt coyotes is legal in your state or province.*

Calls for Coyotes

Either open-reed or closed-reed calls—those that imitate the sounds of cottontails, snowshoe hares or jackrabbits in distress—will work well for coyotes. Coyotes are not as sensitive to volume as many other predators, and calls that put out good volume will sometimes draw coyotes from a half-mile or more away.

While closed-reed calls are easier to use, open-reed calls are capable of producing a wide variety of sounds and are favored by most callers. I do a considerable amount of walking when I'm hunting coyotes, and for that reason I generally prefer to use hand calls over electronic callers. Hand calls are portable, inexpensive, easy to use and dependable; and if you carry several, like I do, you have a variety of sounds at your disposal.

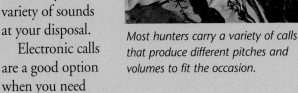

Most hunters carry a variety of calls that produce different pitches and volumes to fit the occasion.

Electronic calls are a good option when you need extra volume—such as on windy days, or when you are calling in an area that has been worked over by other hunters. Tapes provide a variety of sounds that will sometimes appeal to otherwise call-shy coyotes. My favorite "switch-up" tape for coyotes is the sound of a gray fox in distress. This often works wonders when more typical rabbit-in-distress sounds fail.

A howler makes a good change-up to the rabbit-in-distress sounds that most hunters use. Howlers are particularly effective during the January/February mating season when coyotes are claiming and defending their territories. Howlers are also effective for locating coyotes.

—Gordy Krahn

BIG GAME CHALLENGE

Were it not for challenge, there would be little reason to go hunting. It's a challenge to plan a good hunt. It's a challenge to brave the elements. And, of course, the highest challenge of all is to work hard and long to get yourself within bow or gun range of a good animal, and then to make the shot.

From pronghorns on the prairies to elk at timberline—and everywhere in between—big game presents some of our biggest hunting challenges. And in the end, the challenge of it all keeps us coming back for more.

❖ THE SURE-FIRE ZERO ❖

PART ONE OF A THREE-PART SERIES ON IMPROVING YOUR SHOOTING SKILLS: A PRACTICAL TRAINING COURSE THAT WILL HELP YOU SHOOT YOUR RIFLE BETTER IN THE FIELD.

By Wayne van Zwoll

To be of any use, a rifle must shoot where you're looking. The most gifted and practiced marksman won't hit a target or game if his rifle doesn't shoot where he's aiming. That's why it's important to zero a rifle. Zeroing, or sighting-in, simply means aligning the sights with the bullet's path so that the bullet goes where you're looking. You can't change where the bullet goes in relation to the barrel; you can only change your line of sight.

Rifles with iron sights are typically given a rough zero at the factory. That is, you'll probably be able to hit the side of a washing machine at 50 yards without touching the sights. But if you want bullets to hit a smaller target, you'll likely have to make adjustments. Some rear open sights only have a crude step elevator to move impact vertically. Shifting point of impact to the side is a job for a drift punch. Incidentally, you move the rear sight in

the direction that you want the bullet to go.

Receiver sights and tang sights make you more accurate (they give you a longer sight radius than the open rear sight) and faster (they're closer to your eye and obscure less of the target). Almost all of them allow for precise adjustments. Target models have knobs with click detents like windage and elevation dials on scopes.

With the exception of external knobs on target scopes, you move a scope's aiming axis by turning the dials on the turret with a coin or screwdriver. Newer dials have raised ribs or knurled knobs for finger adjustment. Dial "clicks" or graduations are specified in inches of movement at 100 yards. Some shooters say "minutes of angle." A minute of angle is actually 1.047 inches at 100 yards, but it's commonly rounded to an inch. At 200 yards, a minute is 2 inches, at 300 it's 3 inches and so on. Scope adjustments, with quarter-minute clicks, move the point of impact an inch every four clicks at 100 yards, and 2 inches every four clicks at 200 yards. A target scope might have adjustment graduations as fine as one-eighth minute, but most hunting scopes feature one-half- or one-quarter-minute clicks.

Scope It Out

Zeroing your rifle is really zeroing your scope. Start by making sure that the scope is mounted firmly, the base screws tight and that the rings are secured to the base. Before you snug up the rings, make certain that they're aligned. Don't use your scope for this! Dovetail rings are best turned into alignment with a 1-inch dowel. When the scope drops easily into the belly of the rings, slip the tops of the rings over the tube, but don't snug them. Shoulder the rifle to see that the reticle is square with the world and that you have the proper eye relief.

You should see a full field of view when your face rests naturally on the comb. I like the scope a little farther forward than most shooters for two reasons: First,

This four-shot group from the sitting position at 100 yards won't win any competition matches, but it's tight enough for most hunting situations.

Most scope adjustments are graduated in minutes of angle (one M.O.A.=1.047 inches at 100 yards). Each graduation or "click" usually moves point of impact one-fourth or one-half of an inch at a predetermined distance.

when I cheek the rifle quickly, I want the field to open up as I thrust my head forward. I don't want to waste time pulling back to see more through the scope. Often, you'll make a fast shot as with a scattergun, with your face well forward on the comb. Second, I want room between the ocular bell and my eye should I have to shoot uphill or while sitting hunkered over the rifle. I've been bitten many times by scopes set too far to the rear for a stock-crawler like me. My rule of thumb is to start with the ocular lens over the rear guard screw on a bolt-action rifle, then move the scope back and forth incrementally to fine-tune its position.

After you lock the scope in place by cinching the ring screws (alternately, as you would tighten the wheel on an automobile hub), remove the bolt from your rifle and set the rifle into a cleaning cradle or on a couple of sandbags. Look through the bore at a distant object. Secure the rifle, with your "target" centered in the bore. Now take a peek through the scope. If the crosswire is not quartering the target, move the adjustments until it does. If you want the crosswire to move right, turn the dial left—opposite the direction that you'd turn it to move bullet impact. When the reticle is on, check to see that your target is still centered in the bore. Then replace the bolt. Your rifle is now bore-sighted, and you should hit near point of aim out to 100 yards. If Ol' Betsy is a muzzleloader, or a lever, pump or autoloading rifle, you won't be able to see through the breech. You'll need to use a collimator—a device that attaches to the muzzle and puts an optical grid in front of your scope. Adjust the scope to center the grid. Bore sighting is not necessary, but it saves ammunition and time at the range by ensuring that you start shooting with line of sight close to line of bore.

You must still shoot. Don't believe anyone who tells you that a bore-sighted rifle is ready for the hunt or that he has zeroed the rifle so that you don't have to. Always check your bore sighting with hunting loads on paper targets. Always check the zero on a borrowed or second-hand rifle, again with live fire. Even if the previous owner was meticulous in adjusting the sight, you might look at it differently and want a different zero range.

Adjust the Sightline

Because a bullet travels in a parabolic arc, while your line of sight is straight, the two are never parallel, and they can't remain close for long distances. Your line of sight can be adjusted to meet a bullet path tangentially, some distance from the muzzle. But a single juncture robs you of hits at long range. It's better to adjust the sight line to cross the bullet's arc twice—once close to the rifle and again at some distance downrange. The bullet will strike above your line of sight between these two points. That doesn't mean that the bullet rises; your sightline has just cut through its trajectory. Diagrams of bullet arcs can confuse shooters by making the arc appear to rise above the line of bore. It never does. The bullet starts dropping as soon as it leaves the muzzle and continues to drop at an accelerating rate as it loses speed.

Zero range is the second meeting of sightline and bullet path. You can make it almost any range you want with a twist of your scope's elevation dial. But remember that the farther you push your zero, the higher the bullet will strike at midrange. For example, if you zero a 150-grain .30-06 load at 150 yards, it will strike about three-fourths of an inch above sightline at 75 yards. Move zero range to 200 yards, and at 100 steps your bullet hits 1½ inches high. For big game rifles, 1½ inches is still small potatoes. Ignore it. That 200-yard zero increases the distance at which your bullet

Knowing your zero and where bullets will strike at various distances is critical to hunting success. That involves a lot of time spent shooting at short and long ranges.

stays reasonably close to sightline. A 300-yard zero, however, boosts midrange arc 5 inches above sightline, which is too much to ignore.

A rule of thumb for big game rifles is to zero as far out as you can without putting the bullet more than 2½ inches above your line of sight. For most modern rifles, a sensible zero falls between 200 and 250 yards, depending on the load. Your "point-blank range" on big game (the maximum range at which you can ignore bullet drop and hold spot on) will be from 230 to 280 yards, depending on the load. If you tolerate more bullet drop than I do, point-blank range might be longer still. Flat-shooting cartridges let you push your zero farther out. Rounds like the .30-30 Win. and .358 Win., and heavy-bullet loads in the .300 Sav., .308 Win. and .35 Whelen might call for a 150-yard zero. The .45-70 Gov. and .444 Marlin are best zeroed at 100 steps; as are sabot shotgun slugs. Flat-flying bullets from the likes of the .22-250 Rem. and .220 Swift could be zeroed at extreme ranges. This is also true of the 7mm STW and 7mm Dakota, the .300 Rem. Ultra Mag. and .300 Wthby. Mag. But the hot .22s are not for big game. They're called upon to hit rodents—targets the size of soup can lids. A deviation that doesn't matter in a big game rifle can be excessive in a varmint rifle. So most prairie dog shooters use scopes with target adjustments that they can change during the day to keep zero at a range that most shooting occurs. The competitive rifleman zeroes at precisely the yardages that he's to shoot, changing scope settings for different stages in a match.

Your zero is best refined at the bench, with the rifle on a soft but firm rest. You want to remove as much human error as possible. Don't shoot only at short ranges, and consult ballistics charts to see where a zero is supposed to fall. I once worked hard to get a client within killing range of a terrific bull elk, only to see him miss. Another fellow had zeroed the rifle "3 inches high at 100 yards." But my companion hadn't checked it farther out. The flat-shooting Weatherby cartridge showed me a 330-yard zero when I fired the rifle later. It had plenty of reach. But at mid-range, between 150 and 250 yards, where a lot of game is killed, it stuck bullets several inches high. A high hold on the bull's shoulder nudged his shot over the top.

This man's scope mounts were part of the problem. The rings were extra high to ensure that a huge 50mm objective bell cleared the barrel. The higher your rings, the steeper the angle between sightline and line of bore. A scope in low mounts will have a shorter zero range (and less bullet "rise" midrange) than a scope in high rings, if both are adjusted so that bullets hit, say, 3 inches high at 100 yards.

Try It in the Field

Before you take your rifle hunting, check your zero from different hunting positions. The benchrest can't go with you. When you leave it, you leave the firm support that helped guide your bullets when you zeroed. Fire a few groups offhand and from sitting, kneeling and prone positions. You need the practice anyway. If you use a bipod, shoot from it at the range to see if it has any effect on point of impact. I favor a tight sling for field shooting, but I've found that sling tension can pull bullets down as much as 9 inches at 200 yards! A barrel that's not allowed to swing upward and away from a support during recoil, but is instead tugged to 7 o'clock by an unyielding strap, gives you, in effect, another zero. Expect 3 or 4 inches at 200 yards. If the difference is greater, consider changing your bench zero. More and more, I've come to refine my zero from a sling-assisted sit, a position that I use a lot while hunting. It won't give minute-of-angle groups, but I'd rather see a 6-inch cluster around my point of aim at 200 yards than a tight clump in the wrong place. Your first shot at game animals must be very close to where you look.

It's best to zero during a calm day. If you must shoot into the wind, allow for bullet drift, and check the scope with a group when the wind is not blowing. It's a good idea to practice shooting under various wind conditions; however, a windless zero makes correcting for drift easier on the hunt.

A precise zero not only ensures predictability in your bullet's path; it gives you confidence that your rifle will shoot where you look. And that, friends, will help you shoot better. ❖

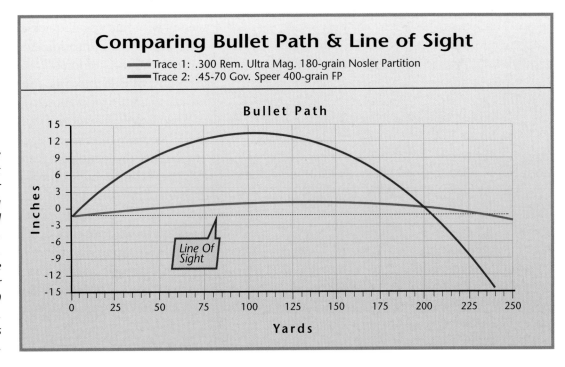

Here's an extreme example of how bullet path varies from your line of sight, depending on what caliber and cartridge you are using. The .45-70 Gov. requires a rainbow-like trajectory to cross your line of sight at 200 yards. The .300 Rem. Ultra Mag. barely rises above your sight plane.

Comparing Bullet Path & Line of Sight

Trace 1: .300 Rem. Ultra Mag. 180-grain Nosler Partition
Trace 2: .45-70 Gov. Speer 400-grain FP

Bullet Path

Line Of Sight

Inches — Yards

YOUR BODY AS A
❖ SHOOTING PLATFORM ❖

PART TWO OF A THREE-PART SERIES ON IMPROVING YOUR SHOOTING SKILLS: HOW TO POSITION YOUR BODY FOR A STEADY, ACCURATE SHOT IN THE FIELD.

By Wayne van Zwoll

It was so easy. The elk stood 80 yards below me, partially hidden by the curve of a hill, but clear of the Douglas fir. Only the lower third of its ribs were obscured by the yellowed grass. I stuck the crosswire on the crease behind the bull's shoulder and pulled the trigger.

Actually, I yanked the trigger, and the reticle dove into the hillside before the bullet left the barrel.

The elk stood still. I cycled the action and sent another bullet on its way. Again I hurried, and the shot

Take the time to get into proper shooting position.

broke high. A drum-roll of hooves told me that there wouldn't be a third chance.

Sad to say, but I've missed a lot of easy shots at game. I have never missed because the scope was off or because a mount screw or action screw was loose. I have never missed because the air was too cold or too warm, or because I forgot to consider the elevation, the barometric pressure or my horoscope. I have misjudged the wind and range on occasion, and in 35 years of hunting have probably hit two or three branches with bullets. But almost all of my bad shots were the result of poor shot execution.

It is easy to miss. Nobody is born a marksman. The mental and physical routines necessary for good shooting are hard-won by disciplined practice. You might be blessed with fine vision, quick reflexes and extraordinary hand-eye coordination. You might have built great muscles and excelled in other sports, but you must still learn how to hold and aim a rifle, and control your breathing and trigger squeeze.

The reason why you don't know many good marksmen is because good shooting comes only after hours of repetitive practice. A crack shot is not someone who kills game consistently (animals are big targets), or who gives one impressive performance (anyone can get lucky), or who gets the smallest groups from the bench (applaud the bench!). The deadliest riflemen are those who whittle group sizes down on paper targets from hunting positions, in time eliminating "fliers." These shooters take care with their positions and technique; firing with sloppy form amounts to practicing bad habits.

A Solid Foundation

Body position is the foundation of every shot. Your body is your shooting platform, and if it isn't solid, you won't shoot as well as you could. The key to a solid platform is using your bone structure. Bones, not muscles, should support you and the rifle. Muscles are elastic and they tire. Muscles contain blood vessels that pulse and nerves that twitch. Bones are like bricks, and if you can align them so that your muscles don't have to work to keep your joints from slipping, you'll build a platform that's as still as the human body can be.

The other thing to remember about body position is that it must allow the rifle to point naturally at the target. If you must force the rifle on target with your muscles, you'll have the same problems as if you depended on your muscles to support your body's weight. As soon as the trigger releases the sear, your body wants to relax. If it is already relaxed, the rifle stays on target. If you have muscled the rifle where it doesn't want to go, it will come off target at the shot.

Shooting Positions

The most stable shooting position is prone because it's the lowest. It gives you the most ground contact and puts your center of gravity just inches above the earth. Your left arm should be almost directly underneath the rifle to support most of its weight. Your left leg should be straight, but it's a good idea to bend or cock your right leg to roll yourself slightly off your stomach. Reducing stomach contact with the ground helps reduce the bounce of your pulse.

Sitting is not quite as steady as prone, but is more versatile when you're hunting because it puts your muzzle above the grass and low brush. It also allows you to follow a moving animal with your eyes and is more forgiving of steep and uneven terrain. It's important to lean forward, with the rear flat surfaces of your elbows against the front of your knees. Muscles in the small of your back will stretch in this position and hold your elbows against your knees.

Kneeling is faster than sitting, but because you're higher, you wobble more, typically in an elliptical pattern from 9 and 10 o'clock to 3 and 4 o'clock. In

competition, the best kneeling shooters keep their backs straight, torso weight centered on the tailbone, which rests on the heel of the right foot. The balls and toes of your right foot bear half of your weight. Your left shin is vertical, supporting the weight of the rifle as your left elbow rests just in front of your knee. Again, "flat-on-flat" is the rule. As with sitting, if you put the point of your elbow on your kneecap, you'll get enough wobble to make you seasick. To minimize horizontal sway while kneeling, turn your left foot parallel with your right leg, which is comfortably off to the side, bearing little weight as it braces your position. Put the rifle butt high on your clavicle, so your face looks forward. A hunched-over position is bad business.

In the prone, sitting and kneeling positions, a shooting sling is a huge assist. I don't mean a strap, which, when you flip it over your arm, tugs at both front and rear swivels, twisting the rifle. A shooting sling (my pick is Brownell's Latigo) has an adjustable loop that pulls taut between your upper left arm and the front swivel, while the rear of the sling remains slack. The result: Sling tension pulls the rifle into your right

A big elk is ample reward for regular rifle practice during the off-season. But neglect practice and you set yourself up to miss.

If you need to kneel or stand for added visibility, try to find a rest—any rest—to steady your shot.

a 30-degree angle to sightline. (I put slightly more weight on the balls of my feet than on my heels.) Your knees should be straight, but not locked. Keep your right elbow high (parallel with the ground) to form a pocket in your right shoulder. Hold the forend where it is comfortable, your left arm almost underneath the rifle. Maintain an erect posture, with the rifle butt high on your shoulder so that you can look straight through the sight without tilting your head. Pull with your right hand; guide the muzzle gently with your left.

A common question from rookie shooters is, "Do I hold my breath?" Well, no. But you do stop breathing, if only momentarily. I generally take three deep breaths (or one, if time is short) as I raise my rifle and align the sight. Getting oxygenated blood to your head improves your vision. I let the last breath out as I take up trigger slack, but I don't purge my lungs. Some accomplished riflemen suggest letting out half the air from your lungs as you start to squeeze the trigger, then locking them. The idea is to eliminate chest movement for the shot while keeping enough oxygen in your body to maintain a sharp sight picture and, if the shot comes late, to prevent oxygen starvation.

Dancing Reticle

Even the steadiest position will produce some reticle movement. You can't guarantee that your shot will break when the crosswire is dead-center on your target, so the next-best thing is to try to make the bullet leave when it is near center. That means applying pres-

Finding a rest that is as solid as a rock will give you a steady sight picture as you prepare for the shot.

shoulder as it transfers muzzle weight from your left hand to your left shoulder. It helps you relax and deadens the effect of your pulse on muzzle movement.

Offhand, or standing, is the position of last resort, because your center of gravity is so high and you have so little ground contact. Because your left arm is not supported by your leg, a sling is of little use in this position—there's nothing to brace your arm against its tension. Good offhand shooters are rare, because you must devote an enormous amount of time to become skilled from this position.

Foot placement is critical for accurate offhand shooting. Start with your feet shoulder-width apart, weight evenly distributed and a line through your toes at about sure to the trigger when the reticle is where you want it, and maintaining pressure when it moves away from that place. Eventually, the rifle will fire. When you become familiar with a trigger, you'll come to know when the shot will go. But anticipating the shot can get you into trouble.

There's a temptation to snatch a bull's eye as the reticle dances through it. A quick tap on the trigger, alas, is hardly ever quick enough. And most of the time it disturbs the rifle, putting the reticle farther from center just as the bullet leaves. Get into this habit and you'll soon be jerking the trigger—a cardinal sin. Discipline yourself to squeeze, and only when the reticle is where you want it. If your muscles get tired before the shot happens, and the sight picture shows increased wobbling, lower your rifle and start over.

As with any athletic motion, follow-through is important in shooting. Keep your eye glued to the target during recoil. Your body will move with the recoil, but if you've accommodated the rifle's natural point of aim, your body and rifle should come back on target. Don't look outside the scope to see the animal's reaction.

Look through it. Keep your face on the comb. Follow-through enables you to tell where the sight was when the rifle fired, so even if you can't see bullet impact, you'll "call the shot" accurately.

Once you know how to make a good shot, there's only one way to become a good shot—practice. Fortunately, you don't have to burn a lot of expensive, hard-kicking ammunition. A .22 rifle costs pennies to shoot and doesn't make you flinch. Another route is dry-firing. You can do this at home, with a black thumbtack on a wall. After double-checking your big game rifle to be sure that it's empty, squeeze off 10 carefully aimed "shots" from each position. Call each shot. When you call a bad shot, try again. A daily dry-fire routine like this will make you a better game shot. Guaranteed! And no, dry-firing does not harm bolt-action centerfire rifles. Avoid it with single-shots like the Dakota 10, and with rimfire rifles. If you're in doubt about dry-firing your pet rifle, ask the manufacturer.

Good shooting doesn't just happen. You have to make it happen. Make your own luck each season. Begin early. ❖

Check your rifle's zero at hunting camp, not so much to ensure that it didn't shift in transit, but to give yourself a boost of confidence.

❖ The Moment of Truth ❖

Part three of a three-part series on improving your shooting skills: Why we miss ... And how to avoid missing. For good.

By Wayne van Zwoll

"Missed one." That's what you'll hear sometimes when you ask a hunter if he got a deer. Don't expect details. If his hunt was successful, your query will trigger a blow-by-blow account of the moment of truth. You'll also get details of the trip, his companions, the old Chevy truck, his handloads, weather forecasts, the state department of wildlife and how things have changed since he started hunting.

A miss, however, he would just as soon forget, and if he admits it to you, he'd just as soon that you forgot it too. A miss signals failure. If there were no deer to shoot at, or if he passed up a buck because he wanted a bigger one, coming home without venison would be

no disgrace. But a miss means that he had a chance and muffed it. You can only imagine how he endured the long stories spun by successful hunters in camp and afterward; tales that, mercifully, are usually shelved by Christmas. You can imagine because you've probably been there, too.

Actually, you don't have to miss ever again. Missing is what happens when you take a shot that you're not capable of making. If you choose your shots carefully, you'll kill every animal that you shoot at.

"But nobody does that," you say. Well, I know people who rarely miss. They're good shots—some are extraordinary marksmen—but what separates them

Everything comes down to the moment of truth: knowing when to shoot, and when not to.

from shooters with less enviable track records is their shot selection. Even the best rifleman will miss often if he shoots at every deer that shows itself. You've seen bucks that flash their tails at 20 steps and then are instantly swallowed by thornapples; bucks running over a ridge far away; bucks giving you but a sliver of vitals in a scope field chalked up by horizontal snow in front of a gale-force wind; bucks standing as still as a post in easy range as your heaving lungs bounce the crosswire from one end of the township to the other. Shoot at one of these deer and you'll likely miss.

These days, I try to limit my shots to those that I can make nine times out of 10.

"Part of knowing how to shoot well is knowing when not to shoot," a friend told me long ago. He was an excellent shot—good enough to have won two Olympic gold medals at 300 meters. "I like to hunt deer. I don't shoot at running deer or at deer beyond 300 yards," he said.

Consider that for a moment. This fellow was, at the time, one of the world's best hands with a rifle. But he only took shots that many of us would call easy. Where does that leave the minions who brag about toppling deer at 400, 500 and 600 yards, sometimes when the animal is on the run?

Once, I fancied myself a pretty good shot. I'd won a couple of state championships and managed a shiny score during an Olympic tryout. Then, in the rugged canyon country separating Oregon and Idaho, I spotted a deer. It wasn't a big buck, but big enough for me that late in the season. I sat down, cinched up the sling on my .300 Win. Mag. and found the buck in the 4X scope. He looked to be 350 yards off, so I placed the crosswire on his back and fired.

Six or seven shots later, the buck lost his footing and rolled down the hill. I collected him at the bottom of a steep canyon and had to backpack the meat to the top. That grind was fitting. I shouldn't have shot at the deer at all. The misses and poor hits proved that I was incapable of getting it right the first time—or the second or third! If you aren't sure of a lethal first shot, it's best to hold your fire. Wait for a better chance, get closer or pass on the animal altogether. It's better to continue hunting with a clean rifle than to miss or, worse, cripple game.

Offhand shots at running game require lightning-fast decisions and immediate action.

At long range, you often have time to deliberate. In the woodlots, where deer come and go faster than shooting stars, you must decide as the rifle flies to your shoulder. Still, you can—and should—abort if the sight picture does not look exactly right. A woodsman who took most of his deer in heavy cover observed that he committed to every deer that he saw as soon as he saw it. "You don't have time to both watch deer and aim at them. You can stop a shot at any time," he said. "Hesitate up front, though, and you lose every option."

That's good advice. Even if the animal is far away and undisturbed, and you intend to get closer, you're smart to get ready to shoot. I often slip into my sling before a stalk. I can't know when unseen game or a sudden shift of wind, or the target animal's random movements will put the moment of truth in my lap. For the same reason, I'm careful not to elevate my pulse to the point that it will prevent an accurate shot on short notice when approaching game.

The things that affect your decision to shoot are the same things to assess in making a shot: range, wind, your position and readiness, and, if the animal is moving, target speed and angle. You might add vertical angle if you're in steep terrain, though I suspect that most game missed "because it was above (or below) me" would probably have been missed if there'd been no elevation difference at all. Incidentally, you hold low when shooting both uphill and downhill if the range is long and the angle severe. Inside 200 yards, with a gradient of 30 degrees or less, forget about vertical angle.

Range estimation becomes a factor beyond 250 yards or so. Out to that range, most popular big game calibers will keep their bullets within 2½ vertical inches of sightline if you zero for 200 yards. At 300 steps, figure a drop of 6 or 7 inches and hold on the animal's spine. At 350 yards, aim a foot above where you want to hit. A 400-yard shot puts your bullet roughly 20 inches low. Naturally, these values vary with the load and rifle. You'll have checked impact points on paper targets before the season. You'll also have put your range-estimating skills to the test, either by pacing or using a laser rangefinder. If you can stay within 10 percent of the actual yardage, you're pretty adept! And the error will be insignificant to 300 yards. Any shot farther than that requires a more accurate estimate, as the bullet path gets steeper.

Wind speed is hard to estimate, and the wind at the target isn't necessarily moving the same speed or direction as the wind that you feel. Ignore a light breeze. If a wind 90 degrees to your bullet path picks up to 10 mph, figure that it will move the bullet sideways about as much as gravity pulls it down at 200 and 300 yards. Wind at oblique angles has a lesser effect. Double the wind speed, and you get double the drift—

but a 20 mph wind is quite strong. To make a killing shot in wind at the moment of truth, you will need to practice shooting in wind. Anemometers like the palm-sized Kestrel will help you estimate wind speed.

Running game is harder to hit than standing game, so I generally pass up running shots. But once in a while I'll succumb to temptation. Because I'm picky about these shots, most of my bullets hit the vitals. The key is knowing how much to lead, then maintaining a smooth swing. To calculate lead, you must know the animal's apparent speed—actual speed mitigated by the angle of travel. A deer running 20 mph across your front has an apparent speed of 20 mph; but if that buck turns at a 45-degree angle, his apparent speed is cut in half, though he's still moving at 20 mph. A deer running directly toward you at 20 mph requires no lead; apparent speed is zero. Next, you need to know the range and how fast your bullet is traveling. Say that the range is 225 yards and you're shooting a 7mm Rem. Mag. Your 160-grain 7mm bullet leaves the muzzle at 3,000 fps. But wait. That's only exit speed. You need to know how long the bullet takes to reach the target, so the average velocity over 200 yards is the correct figure. That's just shy of 2,800 fps. The target is 675 feet distant, and the bullet arrives in a quarter second. During that time, the deer moves about 7 feet (20 mph is roughly 29 fps; ¼ X 29 = 7+). Swing the crosswire 6 feet in front of the shoulder and keep swinging as you fire. You'll shred the lungs.

Knowing where you should hold, alas, does not guarantee venison. You must still tame the reticle and squeeze off the shot without dis-

If you can keep your focus and stay disciplined when your moment of truth arrives, misses will become few and far between.

turbing your sight picture. If you've practiced the fundamentals, you've done this many times. At the moment of truth, you must repeat, with the sudden awareness that your hunt hinges on what you do this second, that the shot will either enable you to tell stories or condemn you to listening. If the buck has big antlers, the pressure mounts, because this deer can make you a hero. If the bullet flies true, you'll be a little bigger than you really are in the eyes of other hunters. You'll earn the spotlight. On the other hand, if you miss, you will have failed in a colossal way. You cannot then say, "It was just a little deer. I was really after a trophy."

Such musings can make you miss. You'll also shoot poorly if you measure antlers before the buck gives them up, or if you let your attention drift to other bucks that pop into view.

In addition to the load on your mind, you might have physical hurdles: cold fingers, stiff muscles, a heaving chest, poor position or rain on your scope lens. Disciplined practice pays off here, with a shooting routine that's automatic. A tip: Always be aware of your feet and shooting alleys. Keep your feet out of any places or debris that might compromise their placement for a quick shot. Keep them well apart for good balance—but not so far spread that they deny you quick rotation to an open shooting lane.

Many hunters miss each year because their mind and body are not focused. To make a killing shot, you must forget about everything except making the shot. Aim for the lungs because they are the biggest of the deer's vital organs. Do not shoot at the head or neck! Keep your eyes off the antlers, because you tend to shoot where you look. Think and act deliberately, but with dispatch. Move smoothly as you tell yourself that you will tag this animal. Sometimes a mantra is in order: "Squeeze, squeeze, squeeze" for instance, or "Make the first one count"—or simply, "Focus."

Good shooting on the hunt starts months before the season, but after you've mastered the mechanics, it's a good idea to prepare yourself for the moment of truth. Your paper targets will tell you how far you can accurately shoot from each position. Timed offhand practice at short ranges will show you if you're up to shooting quickly at moving game. By opening day, you'll know which shots are almost sure bets and which you'll want to decline. If you can bring your mind and body to bear on the crosswire when a good shot comes, chances are good that you'll make it. Remember, you don't have to miss. ❖

Hold low when shooting both uphill or downhill if the range is long and the angle severe.

❖ A Pronghorn Playbook ❖

By Tom Carpenter

Given their druthers, most pronghorn hunters love to pull off a traditional stalk. It's the classic way to get your goat. You know the story:

We walked and glassed a lot. Looked over quite a few bucks. Then, by golly, we finally found Mr. Right on day two! Planned a great stalk. We backtracked, looped far out and around the animals, then approached them from behind a hill, through a draw and finally crawled up a gully. The wind was perfect. I slithered up to the final rise and took a deep breath. The rifle bucked. He was mine.

That's nice. But how often does a pronghorn hunt happen so perfectly? Not as often as we knobby-kneed, cactus-crawling, sage-skulking antelope chasers would like.

Sometimes the animals are just downright skittish: too smart to be stalked. Maybe they're living a mile out on the flats without a sprig of grass or dip of terrain to hide your approach. Maybe you can't even find an animal, let alone sneak close enough to one for a shot.

The wind's not right or it's blowing too hard. Or the goats are moving too fast to intercept. Or the bucks are chasing does and won't stay put. Or snow and rain makes conditions miserable for pronghorn and hunter alike.

Whatever the reason, a pronghorn hunt can get tough. Here's an example.

We were closing in on the last day of the hunt. Wyoming's late-September weather had turned sour,

dropping rain the first day, a rain-snow mix the second. Not only was the weather horrible, but the antelope were extra spooky because of the wind and some recent hunting pressure. My brother, Chuck, and his namesake son had managed a couple of good bucks—we worked like heck for them—but times were tough for poor old me.

The third afternoon found us high on a windy ridge, following a buck and his harem. The snowflakes on one side of the ridge would, when they melted, flow to the Platte and the Missouri and on down to the Mississippi and then the Atlantic; on the other side, they'd remain in the great Red Desert Basin.

Then visibility went to zero. Snow accumulated to our boot-tops. We packed it in and slipped and skidded the truck five miles to find a sagging tent and buried camp. The wind was howling. It was 20 degrees and dropping fast.

We threw the mess into the back of the truck and plodded 30 miles to town and a roadside motel for the night. But lying there in a warm bed, proud of our survival skills (saved by credit card plastic!) there was a gnawing in my stomach.

I had a tag to fill, and a day to do it. I wasn't upset. I wasn't going to gauge my worth as a human being on whether I shot an animal. But I wanted to shoot a pronghorn fairly, on its turf, like I always play the game.

So I drifted off to sleep thinking of my Pronghorn Playbook—a collection of techniques to use when the stalks aren't working, the hunt isn't going quite as planned and it's time for a change in strategy if you're going to get sure-kill close to an antelope.

CHALLENGE: Pronghorns Are Skittish, You Can't Stalk Close Enough

PLAY: Pronghorns off the "Roost"

Work to find a buck or band of pronghorns during

the late afternoon. Watch them through dusk, memorizing the lay of the land and identifying a strategic spot, within rifle range of the animals, to return to. Take a GPS reading if needed. Wake up a half-hour earlier than you think you need to the next morning and walk (don't drive) quietly to the "roosting" spot under the cover of darkness. Set up and wait for shooting light. The pronghorns will be where they were the previous night, or darn close. Take your shot.

You might walk the walk, but you also need to talk the talk when pronghorn hunting becomes difficult.

PLAY: Early Shift, Late Shift

Has someone told you that pronghorn hunting is civilized and that you can sleep in, hunt a few midday hours and then have supper at the diner back in town with the regulars? That's wrong. Real pronghorn hunting is just like other big game hunting: The animals are more actively feeding and moving, hence visible and easier to find, early and late in the day.

Early, as the sun is coming up, pronghorns are less flighty than usual, so they can be more easily approached. During the evening, it always amazes me how I can find feeding, moving pronghorns that must have been bedded or tucked away in the folds of the land all day. Morning and evening, the wind is generally calmer and more predictable, making for better stalking. And you can use the low sun as cover at your back and in the pronghorns' eyes.

PLAY: Get a Good Calling Plan

All stalks aren't perfect. Sometimes the animals figure out that something's up and get nervous, but they don't bolt. So I carry pronghorn calls while I stalk. The sounds can calm and hold the animals long enough for a shot and, in some cases, pull them closer. I carry an Antelope Talk call (E.L.K. Inc.) in my mouth to make the squeals, mews and barks of talking pronghorns. During the rut, I'll wear an Antelope Challenge call from Lohman around my neck to make buck grunts and challenges and try to lure the animals in, or at least put them at ease. Get a good tape and learn the sounds for both calls.

CHALLENGE: Blew a Stalk or Missed a Shot

PLAY: Pronghorns off the "Roost"

If your target pronghorn takes off for the next county, don't despair. Antelope are homebodies. So try this the next time you miss a shot or booger the animals: Find a convenient prairie wash, dip, boulder or other hidey hole, snuggle in and stay put. I call pronghorns "loopers" because within an hour or two, sometimes less, they will often loop around and rebound back to where they started. And there you wait!

PLAY: All is Not Lost

Here's another play for boogered pronghorns: Don't give up! If you don't have the patience to wait for the loopers, head in the direction that they went, sneaking and skulking and looking for them. Circle into the wind if it's blowing, like the pronghorns will. They won't go as far as you might think, before stopping and calming down again. They'll be alert, but are approachable if you plan another stalk carefully.

CHALLENGE: Pronghorns Always on the Move

PLAY: Pronghorn Stands

This is the perfect play for rifle season's opening day or any time when hunting pressure has pronghorns on the move. Or maybe the rut is on, and the bucks are chasing does with a vengeance.

Now is the time to choose a pronghorn stand and wait for your buck. The best stands: travel routes that you see pronghorns using. Good places include saddles or dips in ridges between drainages, points of higher land that project into the flats, and corner fences where pronghorns might bunch up because of their reluctance to jump or duck barbed wire. Hide as well as you can, have your rifle at-the-ready to minimize movement and be still!

On a recent muzzleloader hunt, my friend, James Martin, shot a doe on the last morning using this play. He set up before first light near a fence crossing that we had seen the goats using consistently, and at 8 a.m., right on schedule, we heard one big "boom!"

PLAY: Find the Water

Yes you can, while carrying a rifle, hunt pronghorns that are coming to water. In fact, this could be your best technique if the pronghorns are travelling willy-nilly about the prairie, because they will be thirsty and come to water more than usual. Pick a hiding place on a route to the watering spot and wait for the thirsty runners to come in. They will be on the alert, so stay still. Today's portable fabric blinds are great for this type of hunting; be sure to attach an orange flag for safety and to steer other hunters away.

CHALLENGE: Can't Find Bucks, or Any Pronghorns at All

PLAY: Visit the Does

Sometimes during the course of a hunt you'll locate a group of does without a buck. Don't give this group the short shrift. If it's September or October, the bucks are interested in the ladies and might come calling. While you don't have to follow the does constantly,

Waterhole Bowhunting Play: Prayer

Decoy hunting with archery gear is exhilarating, but sitting in a waterhole blind is still the best way to arrow a goat. Unfortunately, if pronghorns aren't coming in, there's not much you can do other than switch blinds. Beyond that, offering some prayers to the gods of the hunt (who I think we all believe in, at least a little bit) is about all that you can do. It has worked for me. Then it's up to you to make the shot.

it's worth the effort to not scare them. Just let them be, and sneak in to check on them every once in awhile to see if a beau has joined them.

PLAY: Backcountry Bucks

Sometimes you won't be able to find an antelope in beautiful country where they're supposed to be. The solution? Search the backcountry where no one else goes, using your feet to carry you into the rough badlands where the pickup and ATV hunters can't travel. This country is accessible if you just walk a little, and it's amazing how nobody takes the time to work into it and hunt! The pronghorns you'll find here, either up high or in the badlands mule deer country, will reward you with calmer dispositions: You can actually stalk them here ... and the rough, broken terrain helps.

PLAY: Find the Food

Learn what browsing pronghorns eat during the fall (shrubs like sage and bitterbrush, forbs and weeds, not grass) and when they eat (concentrated during the morning and evening), then hunt near the food sources. Especially good spots include natural dips, bowls and basins that catch a little more runoff water. Often, during a dry fall, you can see the green in these spots. That's where to go. Crop fields, too, especially green alfalfa and sprouting winter wheat, will draw the animals if you have private-ranch access, permission to hunt the fields, and to shoot around irrigation equipment.

THE PLAYBOOK IN ACTION

Back to the snow-marred hunt. We awoke the next morning to a temperature of 10 degrees and 30 mph winds gusting upward from there. As we drove to our hunting grounds, I knew which play I was going to start with: "Visit the Does." Over the past several days, a big group of buckless does had been hanging around a nice, protected basin, far from any road or trail. The rut was on. Surely a buck would find them.

We trudged a mile and a half across the sage, first on our feet and then, near the last rise, on our knees, and finally slithered on our bellies through the new snow.

The does were there. And a buck, a good one, had claimed them! We rested a moment, breathing the cleanest air imaginable, then I came back up and nestled into the shooting sticks.

My first shot missed in the driving wind. The buck looked around, not knowing what was up. Quickly, I threw a new cartridge in the A-Bolt's chamber, but the does were milling. When they cleared, I sent my second shot, held to the right against the wind, on its way. The buck collapsed in a heap on the sagebrush turf. The Pronghorn Playbook had come through again. ❖

Muzzleloading Play: Dogged Persistence

Any of the 10 plays will work for muzzleloading hunters as well as rifle hunters, only you have to work harder to get closer. My nephew, Chuck, used the "All is Not Lost" play in southern Wyoming last September. We had spooked a buck, and the teenager wouldn't take "no" for an answer. He crawled a true mile flat on his belly through foot-high sage and thumped the buck from 86 paces with one shot from his peep-sighted .50 caliber T/C Scout. His dad watched the two-hour show while I went to town for a soda, not believing that Chuck would succeed. But he did, against all odds.

PROWL-AND-PULL PRONGHORNS

By Michael Faw

If our nation ever designates a pronghorn capital, Moorcroft, Wyoming, would get my vote. Moorcroft is a quaint little Western town with long lines of noisy coal trains passing through its center. And from the Cozy Motel on the edge of town, you can see pronghorns—plenty of 'em. They often mill around on a hillside across the street. Our hunting party saw thousands of them in the surrounding region during a three-day hunt. I suspected that there might be more pronghorns than people in Wyoming.

So I checked. My reference atlas lists Wyoming's population at 450,000. According to the state's game and fish department, the pronghorn population was nearly 416,000 as of 1999, the latest data available. More than 15,000 nonresidents draw pronghorn hunting licenses in a typical year, and more than 14,500 hunters are successful. A 95 percent statewide success rate certainly helps keep the pronghorns in balance.

Last fall, however, hunters throughout much of Wyoming, including the Moorcroft region, discovered that pronghorns are highly visible against charred black earth—the result of the infamous summer drought and subsequent wildfires. The fire on our hostess's ranch burned thousands of acres of sagebrush. Hunters found that locating a large buck, though, was more difficult, because the drought had negatively impacted the natural forage and, thus, horn growth.

On top of that, try getting close to a pronghorn after it's spent months dodging walls of rapidly moving red-hot fire, noisy bulldozers cutting firelines, ground crews mopping fire hotspots and ranchers repairing—or

Tools for a pronghorn prowl include good binoculars you can use all day, a rifle you know and love, and shooting aids like a bipod or set of shooting sticks.

rebuilding—fences. It had not been a peaceful summer on the plains for pronghorns, and as a result, they were more spooky than usual.

Successful pronghorn hunting required an adaptation to the old spot-and-stalk approach. I like to call it "prowl-and-pull." You had to move constantly and be ready to pull the trigger in a micro-second. Watching water holes was the best option for hunters who did not want to take a long hike.

After prowling several miles through deep gullies and up a steep hill during my first day of hunting, I found a herd of pronghorns hiding under a lone cottonwood tree in a deep valley. Instead of standing in open spaces and using their keen eyesight to avoid hunters, this herd was hiding in the brush like jackrabbits.

I stepped forward and flushed them from the gully. A set of black, pronged horns sliced the horizon, revealing a buck. As he was about to disappear, he stopped to look back. This was a poor—and final—move for him, but an opportunity for me as I lowered my rifle onto my shooting sticks. I pulled the trigger and the pronghorn collapsed.

"Pull" in the prowl-and-pull approach stands for more than pulling the trigger. I had to pull that pronghorn across more than a mile of mountain, then down a thin ribbon of trail that wound its way another mile through the sage to a 4x4 road.

Wyoming is a land of open spaces and long shots, but the often-told tales of 1,000-yard shots on pronghorns were laid to rest on this trip. When our group of hunters sighted-in our rifles, Pat Beckett, Burris Optics manager,

set up a 500-yard target to show us what pronghorns look like—or don't look like—at that distance. I discovered that they are almost impossible to see. Only their shiny, white underbelly reveals their presence when they are bedded.

When rain and the subsequent vegetation return to northern Wyoming, you'll want to go there to hunt pronghorns. ❖

The author helped keep the balance between Wyoming's residents and its pronghorn herd.

❖ ADVENTURES WITH GRIZZLIES ❖

By Bob Robb

A decade of adventures with Ursus Arctos *has led to some interesting and dangerous encounters. Think you're ready to give it a try?*

Mid-October on the Alaska Peninsula is often cold and rainy, and this day was no exception. The foggy ceiling sagged to 500 feet; the air temperature hovered in the 30s—and I was sweating. Less than 100 feet away, a giant Alaska brown bear rolled on his back in waist-high tan grass like an oversized bird dog. I had slipped into position, hoping to arrow him before he knew I was there. I could hear him breathing as he grunted, groaned and gnashed his teeth. The wind was perfect, and only my head and the top of my bow poked over the grass.

Suddenly, the bear stood, and for some reason that I still can't fathom, looked right at me. The sight of my face did not make him happy. He swung his massive

head from side to side, popping his teeth and bunching his shoulders. His first two steps were slow and deliberate, and I carefully let go of the bowstring and found the trigger of the .338 Win. Mag. that I was packing "just in case." At 15 steps, he took a large bound at me. My reaction was a mixture of self-defense and fear. I threw the rifle up like a shotgun, squeezed the trigger and dropped into the fetal position in preparation for the mauling that I knew was only seconds away.

Nothing happened. I stayed rolled up like a frightened armadillo for what seemed like an eternity before risking a peek. Nothing. I slowly sat up, racked another cartridge in and looked around. Nothing. Standing, I saw the bear's unmoving back just above the grass. When I got the courage up to creep over to him, I found that by some miracle the 250-grain Nosler Partition had punctured his throat and broken his neck. He was dead.

I'm not sure how much he weighed, but I couldn't roll him over to start the skinning job without first digging a small trench to one side. I later weighed the hide, with skull and paws still intact on very accurate scales used to weigh aircraft cargo—163 pounds. The hide squared 9 feet, 6 inches.

Oh, yeah ... I tell you without shame that I had to throw my Fruit of the Looms away.

The Magnificent Grizzly

In my mind, there is no more magnificent big game animal in North America than *Ursus arctos horribilis*. Taxonomically, the coastal brown bear and interior grizzly are the same animal. The difference in the two has to do with diet. Brown bears have access to salmon streams and stay outside their dens eating for a longer period of time each year. That's how they get so big. The mountain grizzly has to cover more ground to eat,

A menacing adversary indeed.

subsisting primarily on berries, roots, squirrels, carrion and whatever moose, caribou and sheep it can catch. It's a much tougher, leaner life.

Grizzly and brown bears naturally have a bad attitude. In their world, they are at the top of the food chain and are not shy about letting anyone or anything know it. Fast as a quarterhorse, more powerful than Superman, with a sense of smell that rivals the whitetailed deer, grizzlies are to be respected.

One time I was hunting Stone sheep in the Yukon with a crusty, old sourdough guide. Taking our horses along a riverbottom, we ran into a large mountain grizzly rooting up grasses. When he saw us a couple hundred yards away, he turned and came at a trot. My guide—who was carrying the only firearm we had, because I had my bow—wheeled his horse around and galloped past me as if the starting gate at the Kentucky Derby had just opened. Obviously, it was every man for himself, so I did the same. The bear kept after us for about a mile, then stopped and started rooting again, as if nothing had happened. He wasn't even breathing hard, but the horses were trashed. I think he was just playing with us.

Hunting by the Season

Grizzlies can be hunted during both spring and fall, and there are advantages and disadvantages to each. During the spring, if you catch a bear soon after it leaves its den, the hide is unbelievably lush and magnificent. The trouble with spring hunting, however, is the weather. A freak snow storm and you're out of business. Also, the bears are on the move trying to eat as much as they can. Their food sources are scattered, so you have to cover a lot of ground.

One spring, I accompanied a friend who had drawn a coveted Kodiak Island brown bear tag. The weather was as ugly as it can be for a week, with low fog and rain all day, every day. By day seven we were getting a little growly, as we had not seen a single bear. Then the sun came out, the world came alive, and we spotted five bears in one day. When Paul finally shot a large bear toward dark on the ninth day, it ended up dying in a waist-deep, nearly frozen tundra swamp pond. Trust me when I tell you that standing thigh-deep and skinning a large bear that's mostly covered by icy water is about as

When hunting both mountain grizzlies and brown bears, it is important to shoot the largest caliber rifle that you can handle. However, it is much better to use a lesser rifle that you are comfortable with than a heavy caliber that makes you flinch and shoot poorly. For mountain bears, a .30-06 is my minimum, with the various .300 mags. even better. For brown bears it is tough to beat the venerable .375 H&H Mag., though some folks use .338s, and others jump up to one of the .416s.

The importance of a well-placed first shot cannot be over-emphasized. Three times I have had the "pleasure" of helping clients of one of my outfitter friends trail poorly hit interior bears into mountainside alder patches so thick that I could barely walk through them. Each time the bear has come for us, and so far we've been able to stop him. So far. I wouldn't want to make my living doing this, though.

You need the best breathable rain suit that you can buy (like those in the Gore-Tex Extreme Wet Weather program), as well as waterproof, breathable hunting boots. Dress from head to toe in layers of synthetic fabrics that keep you warm and will dry quickly if they get wet. In some areas, hip boots are necessary. Waterproof, fogproof binoculars from 8X to 10X are essential. Your outfitter (use of a licensed outfitter or guide is required for nonresidents hunting grizzlies and brown bears in Alaska and Canada) can provide you with a detailed packing list.

These hunts are not cheap. Brown bear hunts run anywhere from $9,000 to $15,000, with hunts for interior bears costing anywhere between $7,500 and $10,000. The best outfitters are often booked a year or two in advance. It is important that you carefully research a potential outfitter before any money changes hands.

much fun as hitting yourself in the head with a hammer.

During the fall, bears can be found concentrated on the best food sources. Hunting brown bears over streams teeming with salmon is one of the best ways to take a good bear. Interior bears can be found wherever the berry bushes are thick and heavy with fruit. A popular way to hunt them is to glass mountainsides waiting for one to come along, or to sit over the carcass of a caribou or moose that you took earlier on a combination hunt.

While I love glassing mountainsides and bowls for fall mountain grizzlies, the most interesting encounter I've ever had during the fall occurred in southeast Alaska, while bowhunting brown bears with my good friend and outfitter extraordinaire, James Boyce, of Sitka, Alaska. I was bowhunting, and Jim had a .375 H&H as a backup. We had hiked a mile or so from the ocean, up a small salmon stream that wound its way through the spectacular old-growth forest. The stream bank was covered with bear tracks, but this day we did not see a bear. That is, until we started back to the Forest Service cabin after dark.

A hundred yards ahead and across the stream, our headlamps illuminated three sets of eyes, which could only mean one thing—a sow and two cubs. When the eyes disappeared into the trees and then one set came back out, both Jim and I bristled up. The sow had taken her cubs to safety, and she was back to get rid of the threat. She charged us at full speed, roaring at the top of her lungs like a banshee from hell. She stopped at the edge of the stream—which we both later agreed saved our petunias—and roared some more obscenities. Jim fired twice into the water, but she didn't even flinch. We stared at her until she finally decided that she'd given us enough of a tongue-lashing and retreated toward her

cubs. We couldn't get back to the safety of the cabin and comfort of the bourbon bottle fast enough.

Five Seconds of Pure Terror

I once read that hunting grizzly and brown bears is nothing more than days of boredom followed by five seconds of pure terror. A truer statement has never been made. Often, the hunt consists of nothing more than glassing and waiting in weather that is marginal, bad or worse. Then, seemingly out of nowhere, a bear appears. When it does, the hackles on the back of your neck come to full attention, your palms start to sweat and your heart races. You begin to doubt your courage, your ability to keep your cool and make the shot.

But when you pull it off and sit beside the most magnificent game animal of them all, it's a feeling of euphoria that is impossible to explain.

Try it sometime and you'll see what I mean. ❖

The author, experiencing the satisfaction and elation of a hard, and successful, grizzly hunt.

❖ CALLING ALL COWS ❖

By Mark Kayser

It wouldn't have surprised me to see Santa Claus emerge from the Christmas card-like setting of ponderosa pines and quarter-sized snowflakes. A hazy, brown form sauntering through the white backdrop brought me back to reality. Was it a reindeer leading Santa's sleigh? I knew better. It was mid-September, and I was 3,000 miles from Santa's arctic home.

The raghorn elk poked his head out of the timber, looking for the cows he had heard minutes earlier. Blinding sheets of snowflakes hampered his vision as much as they did mine. He flicked his tongue across his shiny nose while appraising the situation. Since I was only scouting for an upcoming rifle hunt, I let my Sceery cow elk call fall limp on the lanyard and aimed my finger at the bull that was standing broadside at 30 yards. "Bang," I whispered. The bull kept gazing with all the curiosity of a 3-year-old staring at a wrapped present.

A week later, during the season, I convinced a cow elk and her calf to cross an opening using the same cow-calling rendition. A 6-point bull followed, and the

Get the lead cow in a herd of elk moving your way and the dominant bull is sure to follow.

echo of my 7mm Rem. Mag. ended my winter meat worries. It's been nearly a decade since I toyed with those elk, but cow calls continue to receive first-class seating in my elk hunting pack. Calling bulls into range is not a new tactic, but a new twist might be the answer to arranging your next close encounter with a big bull.

Early Beginnings

Modern elk calling dates back decades to the days of tube calls that made shrill whistles, imitating part of a bull's bugle. I remember begging my grandpa for permission to whistle on his Herter's elk bugle whenever we dug through his hunting equipment. I acquired my own bugle from Cabela's shortly after the revolution of using turkey diaphragm calls for elk calls, which was quickly followed by the conception of the cow call by Montanan Don Laubach.

The evolution of elk calling, specifically cow calling, might be regarded as one of the greatest elk hunting advancements in recent years. It altered the way that hunters talk to elk. Still, many hunters find cow calling to be just another way to lure a bull into range. But instead of targeting bulls directly with cow calls, a few elkoholics switched gears to target cows. By luring the herd—led by the lead cow—they found that the bulls would follow.

An Elk Education

Al Morris, a husky elk hunting lunatic from Colorado, opened my eyes to the effectiveness of cow calling after meeting him on a "Cabela's Outdoor Adventures" hunt. Morris eats, drinks and sleeps elk. And whatever you do, don't ask him a question about elk unless you have the day off from work. He has 20 years of elk hunting experience and is more than willing to share it.

Morris began hunting elk in the trophy-rich state of Utah, but today his enthusiasm has him overseeing the outfitting business at the upscale Three Forks Ranch north of Steamboat, Colorado. The property literally crawls with elk, giving Morris that "kid in a candy store" look.

In 1997, Morris's elk calling took a dramatic turn. While at an elk calling championship in Salt Lake City, renowned elk calling expert Wayne Carlton, a Hunter's Specialties pro staffer, pulled him aside.

"Carlton had seen me on an outdoors show and wanted to know why I wasn't using his Fight'n' Cow Call," Morris said. "Carlton gave me a lesson on the spot, using his new call and explained why aggressive cow calling works. I was hooked."

To understand Morris's tactic, you need to understand the workings of an elk herd. Bulls do not associate with herds until just before the breeding season. Prior to and immediately following the September rut, they spend most of their time in bachelor groups. As their testosterone levels increase, antler growth halts, which stimulates them to strip their velvet as their interest in cows rises.

This generally takes place during August. Cows and calves form their hierarchy as they socialize in large herds. This centers around one cow, which the herd looks to for leadership. Her movements lead them to food, water and safety. Where she travels, the herd follows. When bulls join the herd in August, they don't take over the leadership role. Instead, a bull acts more like a security guard. His role is to keep satellite bulls out of the herd, and his sheepdog-like hounding keeps members of the herd from straying. As majestic and dominant as they look, the bulls still follow the lead cow throughout her daily ramblings. This behavior plays into the tactic of calling cows. Get the lead cow interested through conflict or curiosity, and the bulls will follow.

Aggressive Calling

Many experts warn against calling too much, and a "leave your calls at home" mentality has become prevalent in many elk hunting circles. Morris doesn't follow that drummer. He calls more today than he did five years ago.

His strategy involves targeting the lead cow, trying to decipher where she wants to take the herd and making her believe that members of her herd have wandered away and need to be regrouped.

Picking the lead cow out of a herd generally takes a

Place the caller behind the shooter, to divert attention away from where arrows need to be drawn or rifles raised.

few minutes of watching and noting behavioral characteristics. Lead cows have the herd's attention. When she calls, they listen. When she moves, they move. Her mews and chirps overpower other calling in the herd and she has the respect of all subordinates and the attention of the herd bull.

If Morris can visually target the lead cow, he feels

One method of calling cows is using several cow calls to sound like a herd of elk.

more confident because he can see her reaction to his calls. He can then judge if she seems interested, needs additional nudging or is silently approaching.

After pinpointing the lead cow, Morris tries to anticipate her next move. Is she leaving a morning feeding field and heading for bedding cover? Is she trying to lead the herd to water before dropping into a feeding zone? Locating a herd during different times of the day means different calling methods. After weighing the herd's possible movement patterns, Morris moves in for the setup.

Right Place, Right Time

"Success hinges on being where the elk want to be. And much of the time that means intercepting them as they head to food or water," Morris said. "This works well if you know their final destination. Be where they want to be beforehand, then it's easier to convince them that another herd beat them to the goods."

If everything falls together, it's time to get the calls out and become a herd of one. While rifle hunting with Three Forks guide Paul Brown, I found out how easy this is. Brown carries at least five cow calls and an assortment of diaphragm calls to deceive even the wariest lead cows. His varied calls had most lead cows screaming at us to join their ranks. My bull fell to a combination of calling and sneakiness, but I found a new respect for cow calling.

Nearly all major call manufacturers have a lineup of elk calls that imitate the various mews and chirps of a cow, particularly fighting and estrous mews. That's good news, because a handful of calls can easily become the voice of an entire herd if you switch calls and accentuate their varying pitches as Brown demonstrated.

Does Morris leave the bugle at home like many experts recommend? Not on your life. When the cows finally take the bait and meander over, it often takes the squeal of a spike or raghorn bull to get the bull into position, especially when using archery equipment.

Morris recommends beginning with a cow-in-estrus call to target the lead cow. Begin mewing softly, picking up the pace if she seems interested. He backs these calls up with typical herd chatter of conversational mewing. It's normal for the lead cow to take interest since she feels responsible for the well-being of the herd. This might vary from a stroll in the park to an all-out aggressive charge to get the rogue cow back with the herd.

Before the lead cow shows up, it's not unusual for the youngsters in the herd to beat a path to the commotion. Calves and spike bulls often show up first, and it takes patience, camouflage and scent control to allow a herd to pass before getting a shot at the bull. He'll be one of the last animals to pass by, as he follows the lead cow and attempts to keep order within the herd.

If an estrous cow call fails to lure the herd, Morris switches to a lost cow call. Cows use this vocalization to locate a herd or a lost calf. It consists of three high-pitched whiny mews, and lead cows often respond by trying to round up the stragglers. If the lost call fails to spark a response, Morris cranks up the ruckus by switching back to the estrous call, backing that up with a spike bull bugle or chuckle. Using that combination, he's had satellite and spike bulls nearly run him over. His calling setups often escalate to the sound of a frenzied herd, and that's just the way that he likes it. He wants the cows to hear what they want to hear, and he changes calls and sounds based on their reaction and response.

The reaction of the bull dictates how often one should bugle or chuckle. If Morris gets a vocal bull responding, he'll continue to challenge him with bugles in between the cow calls. If the bull shuts up after hearing a bugle, Morris continues to work the cow angle, knowing that a bull will eventually follow the cows into the setup.

Visual Aids

This is when a visual aid will benefit your vocalizations. When a bull steps into a shooting lane, Morris eases a decoy into view. For the lone hunter, the decoy might have to be in place before the elk arrive, possibly causing cows to stare at it too long. But for partner hunting, showing the herd bull a cow decoy almost always guarantees a shot.

"I don't let a bull see my decoy until my hunters are ready to shoot. Then I flash the decoy, hyper call and follow that up with a cow and calf call," Morris said. "As soon as the bull gets visual confirmation, he is convinced that a cow is ahead. I think that a hunter could stand up and do jumping jacks after a bull sees a decoy. It really fools them."

If everything works out, the caller is greeted with a bull staring transfixed at the decoy as an adjacent hunter settles a sight behind the bull's front leg. That view through the sight is better than any Christmas present I've ever received. ❖

Lead cows have control over the herd and its daily routine.

❖ THE OTHER ELK ❖

By Wayne van Zwoll

Rocky Mountain elk get all the glory. In fact, most hunters probably don't even realize that there are two other varieties of elk to be hunted in the Lower 48. If you're looking for a new twist to your elk hunting, Roosevelt and tule elk await.

Not even the guides had seen this elk before. When it stepped clear of the timber, Karl Minor knew he'd not find a bigger one. With eight points on one thick beam and ten on the other, the bull was something out of another time. Karl worked hard to steady the rifle. At the shot, the great elk dropped.

That hunt happened a few years ago near Campbell River, British Columbia. It gave Karl Minor the top spot on the Boone and Crockett list of Roosevelt's elk.

World-record trophies don't turn up very often. In fact, the American elk taken by John Plute in Colorado in 1899 was unbeaten for nearly a century. But a Roosevelt's elk that scores higher than Karl Minor's 396-point bull may even now be lurking where no hunters go. The Roosevelt's is an animal of the deep woods, a half-ton wraith of a beast that vanishes with the dull clump of a hoof or the soft clack of an antler on maple

Named after President and turn-of-the-century conservationist Theodore Roosevelt, this elk is one of six subspecies native to North America.

The others: The American (Yellowstone or Rocky Mountain) elk boasts by far the largest range and greatest numbers. Before European settlement of the continent, American elk inhabited most of its western half. Even then, when as many as 10 million elk might have existed, no other subspecies was so numerous. Nearly all elk transplants, from before World War I to the present, on native Western ranges and in designated elk habitat farther east, have drawn from American elk herds in and around Yellowstone National Park.

Tule elk frequent small areas of coastal California. All but wiped out by settlers during the late 19th century, they were saved by local rancher Henry Miller who, in 1874, set aside some of his land as an elk refuge. Tule elk are hunted now—but lightly. Recent estimates show a total population of fewer than 4,000 animals. The good news is that the herds have been growing steadily.

Manitoba elk grow about as big as Roosevelt elk—which is to say that they're the biggest elk, with mature bulls sometimes scaling more than 1,000 pounds live weight. They once roamed from central Canada south to Oklahoma, but agricultural development has gobbled up their range. Now a stable herd of around 10,000 remains on small islands of habitat (mostly in provincial parks) in central Manitoba and Saskatchewan.

Eastern elk succumbed to early white settlement. John James Audubon, while painting birds during the early 1800s, saw few Eastern elk. Though some would argue that it is not extinct, the subspecies was probably gone before automobiles appeared. American elk have been transplanted to many places that once held Eastern elk.

Merriam elk lived mainly in Texas, New Mexico, Arizona and the Mexican states of Sonora, Chihuahua and Coahuila. Nowhere were they plentiful. Evidently, herds had begun to diminish even before settlers and market hunters exacted their toll. The last Merriam elk sighting occurred before 1906.

The Roosevelt elk survived unregulated hunting in part because of its habitat: dense conifer, alder and maple jungles from northern California to Alaska. Some of this cover qualifies as rainforest; most of it blankets steep terrain. It's easy to spend a lot of time in prime Roosevelt elk cover without seeing a bull.

While British Columbia yields a big Roosevelt bull from time to time, more than 90 percent of the 50,000 elk in that province are American elk. California's token herd of around 4,000 Roosevelt elk is more than double Alaska's. So it's no wonder why hunters go to Oregon and Washington. By recent estimate, Oregon

Roosevelt elk

You need layered, breathable clothing. I like a Filson wool coat, because wet is a standard condition. Prepare, however, for warm, dry weather and for snow. Deep cold is rare. Waterproof boots make sense. My Redwings aren't, but I bring lots of boot grease and an extra pair so that one can be drying while I hunt. Bring lots of socks. Buy top-quality raingear from companies like Cabela's and Browning. Full suits, not ponchos. Binoculars of modest power make sense. A 7X35mm is fine. Leica and Minox 8X32mms tuck easily in rain.

If you're going after elk where they live, carry a short, lightweight rifle with iron sights or a low-powered scope. In my rack is a Remington 700 in .35 Whelen with a 22-inch barrel, wearing a 4X Zeiss scope. Another good choice is the Weatherby .338-06 Ultra Lightweight, with its 2.5X Sightron beside it. If you're stand hunting, you can take longer, heavier artillery with more powerful sights. Stout bullets are best because these elk are big and often taken with quartering shots. Scope caps keep lenses clear in the rain.

Some standard equipment for elk in the thick: wool coat, lightweight rifle and yes, binoculars—to pick out elk pieces and parts.

has nearly 60,000 Roosevelt elk. Washington claims about 30,000—excepting Oregon, more than all other states and provinces combined. These 80,000 to 90,000 animals comprise about half the total elk population in Oregon and Washington, and all live west of the Cascade summit. Some interbreeding with American elk occurs in the Cascade Range (so, too, with black-tailed and mule deer). For record-keeping purposes, Interstate 5, a highway skirting the west hem of the Cascades, is the dividing line.

In Oregon, it's easier to get a tag for Roosevelt elk than for American elk. All east-side, first-season hunts now have tag quotas filled by lottery. You can buy general-season west-side tags over the counter. In Washington, tags for both Roosevelt and American elk are available without application. Of course, the most desirable hunting units in both states have hunter quotas, with permits allocated by lottery. Hunting seasons for riflemen occur in November. Archers and black-powder shooters have other options, beginning as early as August and running into December. Mind the point restrictions on bulls—they vary by unit.

Hunting Roosevelt elk is a lot like hunting any other elk. Camp near the elk, but not where you expect to find them. Elk are mobile and will move from an area that you've disturbed. Get up early so that you can distance yourself from hunting pressure before sunup. Use your binoculars. Yes, even if the cover is thick, you'll pick up more detail with your glasses than with your naked eye. In the forest, focus your binoculars at 40 yards. If you stop at a clear-cut's edge for lunch, refocus. Stay afield as long as you can, moving on elk trails and skid roads.

Bushwhacking is not only hard work—it's next to impossible in some coastal cover—it puts noise and movement where elk don't expect either. Right away they'll know that you're a hunter and they'll slink away. Also, moving off-trail can get you lost. Roosevelt elk live where deep clefts and impenetrable thickets can suddenly force detours. And the tall vegetation won't give you the panoramic Montana vistas so commonly associated with elk hunting. Stay on trails, however faint.

Many rookie Roosevelt elk hunters are confounded by the lack of broad, smooth thoroughfares common in the Rockies. Those paths are established in dry places, where vegetation trampled last week isn't already replaced by new growth; where winters are cold and main routes are kept open by horse and cattle traffic.

In west-side elk country, winters are mild. Rainfall can exceed 100 inches a year. Scuff your toe in the dirt, and something will start growing. There's scant horse traffic through the vine-maple snarls threading Oregon's Coast Range or among the ancient conifers of Washington's Olympic Peninsula. No cattle, either. Those thick places are where the big elk live. You penetrate by winding your way along ground contours marked by tunnels in the alders and places where the ferns and maples see a tad more sunlight.

A trail can disappear where elk have moved off to forage or bed. To find another, you thrash and scramble. "Uphill is best," advised my friend, Vern, who showed me his favorite coverts a couple of years ago. "You just grab anything that doesn't look like a banana-sized slug and start churning."

Level spots are scarce between game trails, and descending makes no sense in cover thick enough to hide a precipice the size of Victoria Falls. So up you go, through mud you wish you'd had as a youngster, and plants with leaves as thick as cardboard and stems like ropes. There's devil's club, too, and salal, the rainforest

equivalent of cactus. You try to be quiet at first. But you finish each day attacking jungle slopes, growling insanely with your rifle between your teeth. Killing a Roosevelt elk exacts a level of dedication seldom found among gentlemen who hunt with dignity from white wall tents pitched at meadow's edge in the Rockies.

You'll rightly surmise that shooting under such conditions can be close. So close, in fact, that many Roosevelt elk hunters don't use scopes. Iron sights work fine where ranges are measured in feet. "Sometimes you get a shot by running after elk," Vern explained. "I did that not long ago, after they blew out in front of me. They were almost close enough to touch, but the brush was so thick that I couldn't see 'em. Well, they hadn't seen me either, and they evidently wanted another whiff of my scent. They stopped, and I burst upon them so suddenly that they stood in shock long enough for me to shoot."

The key, he insists, is to stay with them when they're moving. "Their commotion will drown out any noise that you make. Let 'em get too far ahead, and when they stop, they'll figure you out before you get close enough for a decent shot."

If such tactics sound a bit rigorous, you might want to limit your still-hunting and instead wait for an elk to poke its nose into a clear-cut.

Another hunter, Dale, did that last year. Recovering from recent hip surgery, he had no choice but to sit. And he sat for four days without seeing a bull. Then, on the last morning of his hunt, a herd of elk sifted from cover 100 yards away. The raghorn bull stayed in the shadows, partly hidden by brush and other elk. A group of cows edged Dale's way and bumped into his scent pool. They instantly bounded off, and the rest of the herd moved to join them. Dale's Model 70 was ready when the bull came clear, antlers now plainly visible. He fired as the elk crossed the clear-cut. His .338 Nosler pierced the bull's heart. A just reward for stump-side patience!

Whether you push into the jungles of the Pacific Northwest or wait patiently at their hem, hunting Roosevelt elk will test your fortitude. The reward is worth the effort, though—a chance that the bull you see will have grown big and undiscovered where few hunters make a footprint. ❖

An ... Nolan: "I didn't want to question my guide and outfitter, Nolan Twisselman, owner of Twisselman Outfitters, but the rolling California prairie that we were driving through sure didn't look like any elk country that I'd ever hunted in. "Pardon my ignorance, but do you really think that we're going to see an elk out here? I mean there isn't a tree within five

Tule Elk

miles, and it's all grass." Just about then we topped a small rise and beheld two separate herds of nearly 100 elk — tule elk!

"Ya." Nolan stopped the truck. "I figure we'll see a few." It was the first evening of what was scheduled to be a seven-day hunt, and we'd headed out for a couple hours to check out the flatland portion of the huge 88,000-acre Twisselman ranch. According to Nolan, the biggest bulls held up on the far side of the height of land, where the ranch dropped off severely to the flatlands around Bakersfield. It was late August, the rut was in full swing and, according to Nolan, the odd big bull (an oxymoron where tule elk are concerned because they're the smallest of the elk subspecies) would be hitting the flatlands where the majority of the cow elk hung out. Even without binoculars, I could see bulls chasing cows in the open grassland. Nolan used a window-mounted spotting scope to investigate the bulls further, as he gave me a brief history of the most diminutive elk.

According to wildlife biologists, nearly 500,000 tule elk inhabited California prior to its colonization. As late as the 1840s, there were still huge concentrations of them living in the Central Valley. But by the 1860s, they were, for all immediate intents and purposes, wiped out. Biologists believe that the tragic demise of the tule elk was caused by intense agricultural practices, market shooting and the introduction of non-indigenous grasses by ranchers interested in feeding cattle, not elk.

If these deprivations were not enough, the swamplands, home for the "bulrush" or "tule" in the local vernacular, and home for the remaining tule elk, were drained by the early settlers, further decreasing available elk habitat.

According to Nolan, there were only six pairs of tule elk left in 1874, when Henry Miller, a cattle baron, directed his considerable resources toward protecting the nearly extinct animals. Some sources even had the elk numbers as low as one breeding pair!

By 1905, there were 145 tule elk on Miller's land and, as elk will, they were beginning to make a nuisance of themselves, ruining fences and trampling crops. In 1914, 146 offenders were captured and relocated to 19 different sites in California. Unfortunately, by 1940 there were elk surviving in only three of these areas. And even as low in numbers as these remaining elk were, they were still causing damage to ranches, farms and, according to some reports, even golf courses.

In 1971, in order to address the complaints, the California government decided that it was time to relocate the elk one more time. And so, throughout the 1970s and into the 1990s, tule elk by the hundreds were moved to more suitable habitat. Incredibly, their population grew from 600 animals in 1970 to the present day number of 3,400. In 1987, the tule elk hunting season was re-opened, and in 1998 it was officially recognized as a separate big game subspecies by the Boone and Crockett Club.

In 2000, I was sitting in Nolan's truck looking at a significant percentage of the tule elk population, wondering if there was a big enough bull and just how the heck Nolan expected me to sneak close enough for a shot with my Knight muzzleloader.

"Nothing big enough," Nolan said as he glassed the countryside. "Tomorrow we'll head for 'hell.'"

Nolan was referring to the side of the ranch that fell away steeply to the flatlands of the Central Valley.

"Oh wonderful; 'hell,' that sounds like a lot of fun."

Actually, "hell" wasn't all that bad, other than the tarantulas and blistering 105-degree heat. Spending eternity there would have been relatively pleasurable in light of all the elk that we were seeing. Here an elk, there an elk, everywhere that we looked we would see elk. Early in the mornings, we'd hear them bugling and would work our way closer, trying to pick them out of the thickets on the steep side-hills. Several of the bulls

After crawling to within 100 yards, the author made the shot that put this bull in the record book.

that we located were large, well above the B&C minimum score of 285 needed to make the all-time record book; none, however, would allow me to crawl within 100 yards.

It wasn't until the sixth day that we found a magnificent old bull that wanted to see its picture in *North American Hunter*. After a long stalk and two-hour wait for the bull to come to Nolan's calling, I touched the trigger and sent the Nosler bullet on its devastating way. The bull dropped where it had been standing, less than 60 yards away.

It was a beautiful elk—paler-colored and smaller than his Rocky Mountain and Roosevelt kin, but a handsome animal nonetheless. And to think that tule elk once teetered on the brink of extinction. This is a true trophy indeed. ❖

❖ ELK WHEN THE SNOW FLIES ❖

By Bob Robb

Make no mistake about it—the epitome of elk hunting is the early fall, when the aspen leaves are turning yellow and frosty mountain meadows ring with the sound of the elk's bugle. This is a magical time, and no one who longs to hunt elk should miss it.

However, the bugling period and the often-dead time immediately following the rut aren't necessarily the best times of year to take a monster bull. In fact, they might not be the best times of year to take any elk, be it bull or cow. "Prime time" to harvest an elk is late in the year, after the snows of winter have begun to fall, temperatures have dropped below freezing—sometimes

Tough country, tough weather, tough critter: Tough hunting.

below zero—and the elk have begun moving down from the high country into their winter range.

It's snow—serious, deep snow that stays until the following spring and can reach above an elk's belly line—that spurs the annual exodus of elk herds from the high mountains. In this kind of snow, the elk have no choice. They must leave if they want to find enough high-quality food to sustain them until spring brings forth new grasses.

This annual migration has a profound impact on elk herds. In some high-country areas, elk basically have two home range territories—summer range and winter range. Summer range is much larger and encompasses the high mountain meadows and steep timbered mountainsides. But when the snows come, the elk are forced to lower elevations—flatter ground where they can paw through the snow to find food. Generally speaking, winter range makes up about 10 percent of an elk herd's yearly habitat. This smaller habitat area will concentrate the elk, making them easier to locate.

Of course, in southern areas like Arizona and much of New Mexico, elk don't need to migrate from summer to winter range. In these states, there are fewer advantages to hunting late in the season because the elk can stay high virtually year-round. But when hunting the northern elk ranges, it's wise to consider trying to hunt during the winter migration, if possible.

Migration Hunts

Practically overnight, bulls, cows and calves begin appearing near roads and trailheads and in ranchers' hay fields when the migration begins. No longer does the hunter have to be half mountain man to reach the secluded high-altitude rough country that elk prefer during the general seasons. It becomes easier to find them and, once found and harvested, to get the meat back to civilization.

That's not to say that it's always a cakewalk. Usually you'll end up slogging through snow—often deep

Hunting Migrating Elk

Hunting the late-season winter migration from summer to winter range can be the best time to find a large bull. When the snows get deep enough, the elk will leave the high country near the timberline and filter down through the timbered mountainsides toward winter range. This winter range can be on both public land and private ranch lands, especially those with alfalfa fields. To find elk when they're moving, you can glass from the lowland area, often from your vehicle off public roads. Look for elk and fresh tracks in the snow as the elk begin traveling from timberlines and (A) down obvious game trails (B) and feeding in open grassy meadows and parks (C) located on the timbered mountainsides. Spot the elk late in the evening and mark their location, knowing that they'll be down on the edge of an open park. Then climb to that park in the dark the next morning, getting into position to ambush the elk as they feed into the park at first light before moving on.

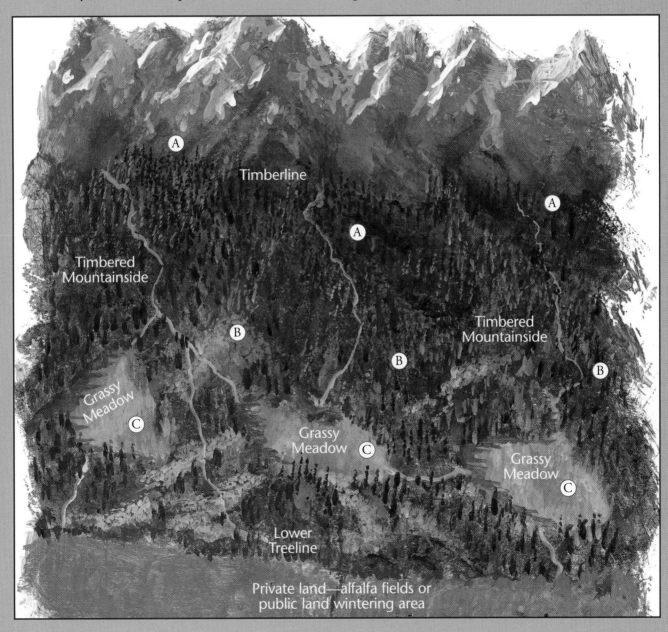

snow—and fighting bitter temperatures and icy winds. But when the elk get closer to the roads, the hunting is always easier.

One problem in hunting the migration is that it can never be timed exactly, like the solstice or the return of the swallows to Capistrano. Elk, however, generally follow the same historic routes every year, and some elk will come down out of the high country during the same time each year. Without the deep snow, though, most elk—and most of the bigger bulls—stay high until forced to come lower.

The amount of snow needed to move elk depends on the distance they need to travel to reach their wintering grounds. If they have no more than a few miles to go, they are more likely to stay high longer. Elk that have to travel 40 or 50 miles—as many herds do—will depart the high country more quickly. As they move, they'll cover many miles each day, often stopping for a few days in small pockets of habitat that have good forage. Again, the amount of snow is the driving force.

How to Hunt in Deep Snow

There are two basic ways to hunt in deep snow.

The first is the standard spot-and-stalk technique. Climb to a good vantage point before daylight, put on your warm clothes and use your binoculars to spot elk as they travel or feed at first light. They often stay out later in the morning now than they do earlier in the fall, simply because they have to eat more to stay warm. This is a decided advantage for glassers.

As for the second way to hunt in deep snow: If I don't find what I want by glassing, I pick up a fresh elk track in the snow and follow it.

This technique sounds simple, but it usually ends in failure. Unless the snow is powdery quiet, the elk will hear you coming. The wind, which can help cover your noisy crunching, must be steady to prevent elk from smelling you. But since the elk is walking and you have to follow his tracks, you can't be choosy about wind direction. Try climbing above the track, keeping it in sight as you follow, which will help you see into the trees and brush and hopefully spot the animal more quickly. Always move slowly in the timber, using your binoculars to glass for pieces of standing or bedded elk. Of course, even if the track is fresh, the elk might be

miles ahead of you, and you'll never catch him.

Cow calling can be helpful when tracking elk in deep snow, especially if you bump them but they haven't smelled or seen you. Often, soft cow calling will draw the herd back, allowing you to pick out an elk to wear your tag.

Where to Hunt

The biggest problem in hunting the elk migration is finding a place to hunt. At present, with the exception of Montana—in which the general rifle elk season runs through the end of November—other elk states close their seasons before the snows have come in strong enough to move the elk. Many states offer special-draw tags for the late season, but they're difficult to draw. Start applying, earning preference points if possible, and keep applying.

Prime areas to hunt during the migration are adjacent to national parks, where special late-season tags allow hunting for elk that are protected inside park boundaries but whose winter range is outside the park. Wyoming's Yellowstone National Park and Alberta's Banff National Park are prime examples. Finding exact migration corridors is as easy as asking a local game warden or game department biologist. These routes are no deep, dark secret, and the officials' objective is harvesting excess elk.

Also, I've spotted many late-season elk from a truck parked on a highway or paved county road, using a spotting scope and window mount to glass long distances into the mountains at first and last light for both elk and their tracks. I like to spot during the evenings. That way, if I see bulls that I want to hunt, they'll usually be close to that same spot in the morning. So I bite the bullet and leave camp many hours before sunup and begin trudging up the mountain in the deep snow, hoping to reach the area where I last saw those elk before first light. If things work out—and they have many times—I spot the bulls as they feed in the same general area first thing in the morning.

Many big bulls are taken by hardy hunters willing to overcome the difficulties of hunting in thigh-deep snow in bitter cold. During winter, when things are right, you'll have the best chance you'll ever have of taking a monster bull. ❖

Most general firearms elk seasons don't open until the rut is over. The odd elk might still bugle. But where the mountains rang with raucous elk talk in September, now all that can be heard are tumbling streams and screaming mountain jays.

The general rifle-season hunter needs a different game plan. It's summed up in one word: legwork.

Scout as You Go

Elk live in small, isolated pockets in a vast sea of good-looking habitat. A large elk drainage might be 100 square miles, but elk might only be living in a handful of places in that entire drainage. To kill a bull, you first have to find one. That means covering country.

Our hypothetical 100-square-mile drainage might be 20 miles long and 5 miles wide. It might also encompass a wide range of elevations. How do you hunt this entire place in a week?

You don't. You scout on the go, splitting the drainage with your hunting partners. Three or four hunters who are in decent shape can cover the entire drainage in two or three days.

Look for elk in small openings in the timber, walking through the semi-open timber across the canyon, and watch for fresh sign. Once you find them, it's time to strategize.

Herd Bulls

After rutting, bull elk—especially the old herd bulls—are tired. They've expended significant energy breeding and protecting their harems from satellite bulls, often losing a quarter of their body weight. Your scouting efforts might produce lots of elk, but they'll more than likely be cows, calves and young bulls.

Once the rut is over, herd bulls are ready to resume bachelorhood. They often find isolated pockets of deep cover where they can rest without being disturbed.

You can find these pockets in the dark timber, among blow-downs and other hellhole cover; on small benches notched into the sides of steep, brushy ridges; near high-mountain saddles; on thick creek- and river-bottoms; and in other nasty, inhospitable places.

Plan Carefully

Once you've found the elk, you must plan carefully before making your move. If you spook them with your scent, careless walking and talking, or poor shooting, chances are they'll move several miles. Then you'll have to start over again.

When approaching the elk, make sure that all hunters have cover to hide behind as they move in. Never underestimate an elk's eyesight, especially its ability to spot a careless hunter out in the open with the sun shining on him. Try to move in from either the same elevation as the elk or, ideally, a bit above them. If you're trying a drive—and small drives can work well, especially if you've scouted the area and found places that make natural funnels for escaping elk—place the standers to cover these escape routes and, if you have enough people, a stander to cover any back-door escapees. The drivers should actually still-hunt, doing their best to slip up on the herd, pick out a bull and get a shot before he ever knows what hit him.

Remember, too, that while elk like to bed in the same general area day after day, they won't necessarily bed in exactly the same place day in and day out. So before you move in on them, it's always better to try to spot them first with your optics.

Index